# THE BUSINESSMAN
# IN LITERATURE:
# DANTE TO MELVILLE

# THE BUSINESSMAN
# IN LITERATURE:
# DANTE TO MELVILLE

## Michael J. McTague

Philosophical Library
New York

to my mother and father

"Most of the luxuries, and many of the so called comforts of life, are not only not indispensable, but positive hinderances to the elevation of mankind."

Henry David Thoreau, *Walden*.

# TABLE OF CONTENTS

# ACKNOWLEDGMENTS

I wish to thank Professor Robert Lindsay of the Finance Department of New York University and Professor Norman Martin of the Management Department for their assistance in the production of this book. Special thanks are due Professor Martin for suggesting the idea.

I am also indebted to my wife, Rose, and to Carol Krob, who also did the four drawings used in the text, for making many valuable suggestions on this topic.

# CHAPTER ONE

## Introduction

This book is intended to be of use to the literary scholar and to the business student. So far as I have been able to determine, there has been no other book, article, or thesis that has attempted as complete a study of the image of the businessman in literature. Within the limits of this undertaking, I have written four separate chapters. The first treats Dante, and three of the major Middle English poets — Chaucer, Gower, and Langland. Old English literature and the Gawain poet present no useful material for this study. The second chapter investigates three major works from the sixteenth and seventeenth centuries: William Shakespeare's "The Merchant of Venice," Christopher Marlowe's "The Jew of Malta," and John Milton's "The Ready and Easy Way to Establish a Free Commonwealth." Chapter three looks at short essays by Joseph Addison and Richard Steele; Jonathan Swift's *Drapier's Letters,* and several occasional poems; Oliver Goldsmith's "The Deserted Village" receives fuller treatment; there is a general consideration of Adam Smith, *The Wealth of Nations,* and *The Theory of Moral Sentiments;* and Edmund Burke's *Reflections on the Revolution in France.* The fourth chapter analyzes Herman Melville's "Bartleby the Scrivener: A Story of Wall Street."

1

Although many recent works would have been appropriate, this study concentrates on Dante and the best known English authors from Old English through the eighteenth century. It is my intention to continue my investigation beyond the works studied here, which, it is hoped, provides the groundwork for further chronological research by focusing on the development of the businessman in pre-nineteenth century works. During the nineteenth and twentieth centuries, businessmen have appeared more frequently in literature. Through the eighteenth century, however, the businessman was not a major literary figure. I have been unable to find any evidence of the businessman as an important consideration in the works of Philip Sidney, Edmund Spenser, John Donne, John Dryden, and Andrew Marvell. The volume of literature studied in this book is not as large as one might suspect, but the absence of suitable material is in itself significant.

The businessman should be concerned with the image of the businessman in the arts. There is, I believe, a drive within business to humanize business. Before teaching management at New York University, Peter F. Drucker taught politics and philosophy at Bennington College. In *The Effective Executive,* Drucker mentions playwright Robert Emmet Sherwood as an effective administrator at the Office of War Information during World War II.[1] David Ewing borrows freely from the humanities in his writing. The "Index" to *The Managerial Mind* lists Shakespeare once, and "King Lear" twice.[2] John Milton is listed five times in the "Index" to *Freedom Inside the Organization.*[3]

Arnold J. Toynbee in *A Study of History* says that if you wish to "ascertain the limits of any particular civilization in space or time the esthetic test is the surest as well as the subtlest."[4] There has been a growing involvement of business in the arts. Arnold Gingrich reported in a 1969 book: "As early as 1939 I.B.M. wisely established a Department of Arts and Science to develop and coordinate extensive programs in support of the fine arts."[5] This evidence suggests that business and the arts are not as opposed to each other as is sometimes supposed. An interesting example of success in business and art together is Pulitzer Prize winning poet Wallace Stevens, who became Vice President of the Hartford Accident and Indemnity Co. in 1934.

I have alternated my method of investigation from close reading to general discussion. In the cases of "The Deserted Village" and "Bartleby the Scrivener," tone and mood are very important in drawing conclusions about the image of the businessman. Adam Smith and Edmund Burke were treated in reference to their overall attitudes toward business.

Other issues are treated from time to time. The attitudes of the Franklin and the Merchant toward marriage are analyzed in some detail. The importance of anti-Semitism in the characterizations of Shylock and Barabas and the tradition of sentimentality are other topics referred to at some length. These discussions, I feel, are necessary to avoid a literal-minded analysis of the businessman in literature.

On occasion the businessman, personalized, is not dealt with, and more general references to business or to merchants are looked into. In the Medieval works included, and in Smith, Burke, and Milton, an abstraction of the businessman can be obtained only by reference to discussions of "business."

Finally, I have concentrated on the original literature throughout this work. References to secondary sources are limited, and are used, for instance, to explain technical terms, and are not the watershed of my analysis. I have tried to do this work with a spirit of scholarship as I understand it, i.e., I have started with the literature, and formed my abstractions from a combination of the literature and my understanding. I have not been squeamish about using the first person, nor about making analogies that I feel could be useful to businessmen.

A brief statement on the major components of my understanding of business and literature is in order. This book follows a Ph.D. in English and a Master of Business Administration in finance. I am presently employed by a training and consulting firm, giving me the perhaps unusual perspective of one who is a businessman and literary scholar. One of my objectives in writing this book was to increase my own understanding of how and why writers have framed their impressions of businessmen. By sharing my efforts with literary scholars and businessmen, I hope I can contribute to a neglected area of literary study and an awakening need in the American business community.

# Footnotes

[1]Peter F. Drucker, *The Effective Executive* (New York: Harper & Row, Publishers, 1967), p. 58.

[2]David W. Ewing, *The Managerial Mind* (New York: The Free Press, 1964).

[3]David W. Ewing, *Freedom Inside the Organization* (New York: E. P. Dutton, 1977).

[4]Arnold J. Toynbee, *A Study of History,* an abridgement of Volumes I to VI by D. C. Somervell (New York: Oxford University Press, 1947), p. 241.

[5]Arnold Gingrich, *Business and the Arts: An Answer to Tomorrow* (New York: Paul S. Ericksson, Inc., 1969), p. 80.

# CHAPTER TWO

## Medieval Views:
## Dante, Chaucer, Gower, Langland

In investigating the businessman in Medieval literature, I have concentrated on four major works, three of which are English: Dante's *La Divina Commedia,* John Gower's *Confessio Amantis,* William Langland's *Piers the Plowman,* and Chaucer's *The Canterbury Tales.* Only *The Canterbury Tales* actually has characters who could be called businessmen; the other three refer to merchants generally, and to the moral questions that surround merchants. Dante's *La Divina Commedia* was probably composed in the years 1315-1321.[1] Although Dante was not a slavish imitator, his work incorporates the major theological beliefs of the Middle Ages. In the words of John D. Sinclair:

> He was a great interpreter and a supreme imaginer, bodying forth the abstractions of scholastic thinking, turning them to shapes and giving them a local habitation and a name . . .[2]

John Gower, William Langland, and Geoffrey Chaucer all wrote in the latter part of the fourteenth century. *Confessio Amantis,* which means "the confession of a lover," is a penitential dialogue between the lover and Genius, the priest of love, incorporating

5

the Seven Deadly Sins. There are forty extant manuscripts of the work, and Gower was considered Chaucer's equal through the sixteenth and perhaps the eighteenth century. Sir Philip Sidney equated Chaucer and Gower in "The Defense of Poesie,"[3] and Shakespeare professes his indebtedness to Gower in his play "Pericles."[4] Since then, Gower's popularity has declined sharply, and he is often accused of "unrelieved earnestness."[5] *Piers the Plowman* is a complex work which involves penitence, dreams, and allegory. It is as morally earnest as *Confessio Amantis*: ". . . Piers Plowman became an accepted synonym for a plain man who makes it his business to act with integrity and to guide others to a knowledge of truth."[6] Chaucer's *The Canterbury Tales,* which survives in 90 manuscripts, is, by present tastes, the finest of the three English works included here. Among other tributes, George Lyman Kittredge said, "Geoffrey Chaucer is nearer to us than Alexander Pope,"[7] and Neville Coghill called him "our greatest comic poet."[8]

*La Divina Commedia* is divided symmetrically into *Inferno, Purgatorio,* and *Paradiso,* or hell, purgatory, and heaven. In *Inferno* the closest representations of businessmen to be found are usurers. The general scheme of Dante's hell begins with *"Questi sciaurati, che mai non fur vivi"* (III, 64), the neutrals. There are three major classifications after the neutrals, arranged according to increasing evil: 1) incontinent, 2) violent, 3) fraudulent. Under "violent," there are three categories:

1. Violent against others,
2. Violent against self,
3. Violent against God, nature, and art.

"Fraudulent" is divided into simply fraudulent and treacherous. The usurers are found between the violent and the fraudulent. In the general category of the violent against God, nature, and art there are three groups: blasphemers, sodomites, and usurers. Usury is considered by Dante a sin against industry, which Sinclair calls a grandchild of God (p. 189). All three of these groups are punished by a rain of fire and scorched earth because this is how God exacted direct vengeance on Sodom and Gomorra (Genesis, XIX, 23-25). The earth is entirely barren here too. In trying to defend themselves from the fire, the usurers are likened to dogs pestered by fleas in the summer. In addition, a pouch hangs from the neck of each usurer on which their gazes are fixed, indicating an avaricious desire for wealth, wholly unattainable in hell.

Usury is fraud because, to Dante, it was benign in appearance, but evil in its intent. This seems not to include reasonable interest charges; usurers to Dante charged excessive interest in a fraudulent manner. A modern equivalent would be a loanshark. Just before Dante the traveller and Virgil, his guide, reach the usurers they confront Geryon:

> La faccia sua era faccia d' uom *giusto*,
> tanto *benigna* avea di fuor la pelle,
> e d' un serpente tutto l'altro fusto.
> (XVII, lines 10-12)

Two words are italicized which indicate the nature of fraud. *Giusto* means true or just; Singleton translated *benigna* as "gracious," Binyon as "mildness." This appearance hides his evil intent. Singleton's note on the canto says, "fraud is the deliberate use of the distinctively human powers for inhuman ends" (page 222).

The important question for our purpose is what constituted usury for Dante. The arms on the pouches around the necks of usurers represent the arms of several well-known Florentine and Paduan families. One reference is generally agreed to refer to Gianni di Buiamonte de' Becchi, who was the head of a money-lending family.[9] These are open indictments, roughly comparable to naming the big seven New York banks. This suggests the view of D. Mantovani that "he seems to have regarded as sinful the mere fact of living and profiting by the lending of money."[10] However, Singleton goes on to say,

> But what he had in view, plainly, was the practice of oppressive and unscrupulous usury on the part of men of rank and wealth, which he reckoned a breach of the social bond of industry, 'God's grandchild', and as a kind of blasphemy to be punished with fire. It was in a

7

special sense the anti-social use of the intelligence, and for Dante sins are base in the measure in which they are anti-social (pages 222-223).

The fraudulent nature of the transaction seems to have been the most important thing to Dante. The first two references to "usury" in *The Oxford English Dictionary* associate usury with thievery and secretiveness. Generally speaking, any interest charged for the use of money seems to have been regarded as evil before the later Middle Ages. The word usury derives from the Latin verb *utor*, which means "to use."[12] It is hard for a modern reader to understand why charging interest was regarded as evil in the Middle Ages.[13] Perhaps the best answer is that money lending was a developing profession, practiced at first by the greediest parts of Florentine society. There were numerous raids for plunder conducted by Italian cities in the Middle Ages. Historian Friedrich Heer, commenting on these raids, calls them a "dangerous legacy to Western Europe as a whole," and refers to the Byzantine view of "the 'avaricious', 'war-mongering', 'unscrupulous' West."[14]

It is also true that for Dante "The moral significance of the commonwealth forms a part of his religion."[15] Dante was personally involved in the political turmoils of Florence. In 1302 he was exiled from Florence, and was condemned to death. He died and is buried in Ravenna. He had a particular reason for hating those involved in running Florence in any way he disapproved of. In addition, there are three people mashed eternally in Satan's three mouths at the bottom of hell: Judas, Brutus, and Cassius. All three disturbed the divine order. Usurers were regarded by Dante as violent against God's natural law. Lest one think that Dante was being petulant in viewing usurers as evil, he presents his personal reactions as a traveller through hell, separate from his understanding of where these sins stood in God's system of punishment. Several times Virgil, his guide, admonishes him against feeling sorry for sinners. Dante's personal reactions do cover a wide range: he fells sorry for Paolo and Francesca (Canto V, lines 109 ff.), and for Ser Brunetto, his teacher (Canto XV, line 30); in Canto XXXII, he kicks Bocca in the face (lines 73 ff.). In the case of the usurers, his reaction seems to be one of contempt,

8

One of Dante's Usurers

not speaking to anyone, indicating that he regarded them as unworthy of anger. In addition, their family arms, which represented wealth, power, and dignity on earth, are instruments of their torture here.

*Purgatorio* might be described as a moral reform-school for saved souls, who have not directed their lives properly toward God. Following an ante-Purgatory, the seven levels of purgation are organized around the seven Deadly Sins. Above these terraces is the earthly paradise.[16] The scheme of the Seven Deadly Sins had been established by the time Dante wrote *The Divine Comedy*. The Fourth Lateran Council (1215-16) obliged Christians to receive the sacrament of Penance at least once a year: a great number of manuals followed, intended to instruct priests and penitents in the Seven Deadly Sins and penance. The Pope who headed the Fourth Lateran Council, Innocent III, wrote *De miseria humanae conditionis,* which is a devastating attack on the sins of the flesh. Major works in the Seven Deadly Sins tradition include *Summa Casuum Poenitentiae* (c 1235) by Raymond of Pennafort; *Summa de Vitiis* and *Summa de Virtutibus* (before 1201) by Guillaume de Perrault; and *Somme de Vices et Vertus* (1279) by Frere Lorens.[17] It is difficult for modern readers to believe that *The Prick of Conscience,* a moral work which uses the Seven Deadly Sins tradition, was the most popular work of the fourteenth century — attested to by its 100 manuscripts. The entire tradition of the Seven Deadly Sins pervades Medieval and Renaissance literature, and provided the framework of a good number of works, such as Chaucer's "Parson's Tale," William Langland's *Piers the Plowman,* Gower's *Confessio Amantis,* and Book I, Canto IV of Spenser's *The Fairie Queene.* Within this tradition, the established pattern, in order of increasing seriousness is, 1) lust, 2) gluttony, 3) avarice, 4) sloth, 5) wrath, 6) envy, 7) pride.

The sin under which usury is treated is avarice, the fifth most evil of the seven. *Il Purgatorio* does not mention merchants specifically, and there are no usurers here; usurers are in hell, damned forever. In purgatory, Dante presents us with avaricious people who are being reformed. Both good and evil attitudes toward money are considered in Canti XIX and XX. The sins of lust, gluttony, and avarice are treated in *Il Purgatorio* as excessive love of earthly things. Dante meets Pope Adrian V, who describes the method of purgation for the avaricious:

> Si come l' occhio nostro non s' aderse
> in alto, fisso alle case terrene,
> Cosi' giustizia qui a terra il merse,
> Come avarizia spense a ciascun bene
> lo nostro amore, onde operar perdesi,
> Cosi giustizia qui stretti ne tene,
> ne' piedi e nelle man legati e presi;
> e quanto fia piacer del giusto sire,
> tanto staremo immobili e distesi.
> (Canto XIX, lines 118-126)

At night, the avaricious recall well-known classical and Biblical examples of avarice: Pygmalion, Midas, Crassus, Achan, Ananias and Sapphira, and Heliodorus.[18] All three Biblical examples concern people who acted out their avaricious desires secretly, and tried to cover their actions by fraud. As noted above, these are the qualities associated with usury by Dante and other medieval writers.

In addition to examples of avarice, the penitents recall examples of generosity — the opposite of avarice. One example is Saint Nicholas, the inspiration for Santa Claus. From the *Aeneid*, there is Fabricius, who was even in classical times "famous especially for his incorruptible integrity, and was a model of plain and simple living."[19] He is treated by Dante as a Roman pagan saint, who chose *uirtute "con poverta"* (Canto XX, line 26), instead of *"gran ricchezza . . . con vizio"* (line 27).

It would be a considerable overstatement to say that either Dante or the medieval church condemned wealth in and of itself. In the case of Fabricius he had virtue and poverty. In the case of the usurers in *The Inferno*, they sought wealth but with evil intent. The medieval position was that wealth implied additional obligations, and that there was a natural temptation for the wealthy to be avaricious, but it was not impossible to be wealthy and generous. Innocent III wrote, "As it is difficult to be in the fire and not be burnt so it is difficult to have riches and not love them."[20] The usurers are seen as wholly fraudulent, evil people.

11

The avaricious love wealth, but they have not perverted God's natural law; hence, their intent was less evil than that of the usurers.

Whereas *The Divine Comedy* was written in the early fourteenth century (Dante died in 1321), John Gower's *Confessio Amantis* was completed near the end of the fourteenth century — apparently in 1390.[21] The work is organized around penance and the seven deadly sins; the fifth book treats avarice, which occupies the same position relative to the other sins that it had in *Il Purgatorio*. Usury is treated within Book V. Gower gives his analysis of the evil in usury very directly:

> Usure with the riche duelleth,
> To al that evere he beith and selleth
> He hath ordeined of his *sleyhte* . . . skill, trickery
> mesure double and double weyhte:
> Outward he selleth be the *lasse*, . . . less
> And with the more he makth his *tasse* . . . heap
> Wherof his hous is full withinne.
> (Lines 4395-4401)

Here the usurer is described as rich, a trickster, who keeps his thumb on the scale, and who piles up wealth by cheating. This particular description does not include interest charged on a loan, but implies that usurers are fraudulent businessmen in a more general sense. As with Dante, evil intent, particularly deceit, are present here. Gower goes on to say that the usurer's "love is al toward himselve" (line 4404), which suggests a lack of love of God and fellow man. Gower is more explicit than Dante about excessive interest charged by usurers:

> For wher he schal oght yive or lene,
> He wol ayeinward take a *bene*, . . . bean
> Ther he hath lent the smale *pese*. . . . pea
> (Lines 4407-4409)

Following his purpose of using illustrative stories concerning sins, Genius tells the story of Echo to illustrate usury in love. The story was borrowed from Ovid's *Metamorphoses,* in which Echo

12

talked incessantly at Hera while Zeus was sporting with nymphs in the shade. Gower changes the nature of the story somewhat. Here Echo is guilty of concealing what she should have told, and in punishment she tells everything she hears, and conceals nothing. This element of fraud is again connected with usury. Basic also to Gower's version of the story is the contract, *borcage,* which Echo arranges.

> Brocours of love that deceiven,
> No wonder is thogh thei receiven
> After the wrong that thei decerven;
> For whom as evere that thei serven
> And do plesance for a whyle,
> Yit ate laste here oghne guile
> Upon here oghne hed descendeth,
> Which god of his vengance sendeth
> (Lines 4573-4580).

Similar also to Dante is the idea that God's vengeance is directed against usurers.

In William Langland's *Piers the Plowman,* there is a description of the personified sin of avarice, which is harder on businessmen than either *The Divine Comedy* or *Confessio Amantis.* Avarice is a cheater in many types of business dealings, and is a usurere: "wickedliche to weye • was my furst lesson" (C. VII, line 210). There seems to be a general assumption that all merchandising involves cheating:

> To Wy and to Winchester · ich wente to the faire
> With many maner marchandises · as my maister
> heghte;
> Ne hadde the grace of gyle · gon among my ware,
> Hit hadde ben unsold thys seven zer · so me god
> helpe!
> (C. VII, lines 211-214).

A key expression here is "the grace of gyle." *Gyle* is translated by Skeat as "deceit, fraud;" and he points out the irony by contrast to the expression "by the grace of God." Avarice goes on to confess various methods of stretching cloth, short weighting, and of selling thin ale.²² He also knows how to mix merchandise and put the poorest quality material in the middle (lines 259-261). In addition to cheating in business matters, the avaricious are accused of failing to love God:

> An yf ich sente over see · my servant to Brugges,
> Other in-to Prus my prentys · my profit to a-waite,
> To marchaunde with monye · and maken here
>     exchaunge,
> Myghte nevere man comforty me · in the meyn tyme,
> Neither matyns ne masse · ne othere manere syghtes,
> And nevere penaunse performede · ne *paternoster*
>     syede,
> That my mynde ne was · more in my goodes
> Than in godes grace · and hus grete myghte.
> *Ubi thesaurus tuus, ubi et cor tuum.*
> (C. VII, lines 278-286).²³

Businessmen who are preoccupied with business cannot concentrate on prayer. The Latin quotation is from Matthew, VI, 21, and means, "For where thy treasure is, there also will thy heart be." This is a very serious indictment for a medieval writer. Repentance, to whom Avarice is telling this, says he cannot forgive Avarice's sins until he makes restitution; Avarice needs a complete change of heart. Later in the poem we have another reference to the difficulty merchants face in seeking forgiveness for sins:

> Marchans in the margine · hadden menye zeres,
> Ac *á pena et á culpa* · Treuthe nolde hem graunte;
> For thei holden nat here halydaies · as holychurche
>     techeth,
> And for thei swere by here saul · and 'so god me
>     mote helpe!'
> Azens clene conscience · for couetyse of wynnyng.
> (C. X, lines 22-26).

These merchants failed to keep holydays, blasphemed, and were filled with avarice.

Usury receives severe treatment in *Piers the Plowman*. Usurers are worse than whores (C. VII, lines 306-7), and they must leave their merchandise and think of God's mercy (line 340). Langland had associated avarice and usury more closely than either Dante, who stressed wealthy families, or Gower, who employed a classical myth.[24]

Of the four writers to be considered in this chapter, Geoffrey Chaucer is probably the best known to and best loved by English-speaking audiences. The tradition of the Seven Deadly Sins does not appear to have provided the characterizations for Chaucer's pilgrims in *The Canterbury Tales*. It seems rather that: "The sketches were divided to provide representatives of the chief classes of English society under the higher nobility."[25] The one place in which the Seven Deadly Sins is used most directly is in "The Parson's Tale," which Kittredge calls "everyday theology" (page 10). "The Parson's Tale" gives much of the kind of material that appears in other works on penance and the Seven Deadly Sins mentioned earlier, but businessmen do not occupy a large place in the Parson's discussion of avarice, and he makes a sharp distinction between good merchants and bad merchants:

> Of thilke bodily marchandise that is leveful and honest is this: that, there as God hath ordeyned that a regne or a contree is suffisaunt to hymself, thanne is it honest and leveful that of habundance of this contree, that men helpe another contree that is more nedy. / And therfore ther moote been marchantz to bryngen fro that o contree to that other hire marchandises. / That oother marchandise, that men haunten with fraude and trecherie and deceite, with lesynges and false othes, is cursed and dampnable.
> (Lines 778-780)

Bad merchandising is connected with treachery and deceit again. Chaucer's Parson has much to say about lords and their bondsmen (753-774) and about simony, but usury is not mentioned. There are a number of possible explanations for this. One is that Chaucer chose not to consider usury separately from avarice, meaning it to be included in the general topic. A second is that usury had become a muddled topic — hard to distinguish from honest business dealings: the rise of the merchants had created new financial demands. A third possibility is that Chaucer had personal reasons for leaving usury out, and for including a clear reference to honest businessmen. It is believed that Chaucer's father, grandfather and stepgrandfather were wine merchants.[26] In addition, Chaucer was connected personally to many wealthy men who might have been offended by a lengthy discussion of usury. A fourth explanation is that he was more concerned with simony and extortion, and did not bother to make extended comments on usury. Chaucer seems to be hardest on the Summoner, the Pardoner, and the Friar, because they all pervert their sacred responsibilities. Usurers may not have been regarded by Chaucer as the most evil people.

Usury aside, we can assume that all four of these writers understood that merchants could be either good or bad. If a merchant were evil, avarice would be his most likely sin, usury being one form of it. Although *Piers the Plowman* was harder on merchants than the other works discussed so far, it should be remembered that each of these works has a penitential theme. The seriousness of these sins was enormous: "For know this and understand, that no fornicator, or unclean person, or covetous one (for that is idolatry) has any inheritance in the kingdom of Christ and God" (Ephesians V, 5). The preacher's job was to make his hearers aware of their sins, so that they could know them and repent with clear consciences. The treatment of merchants as indicative of avarice resembles the general association of other professions and entertainments with sins. "The tavern . . . was considered a center of vice and debauchery. It was the target of many a sermon."[27]

In addition to the rather brief treatment of avarice in "The Parson's Tale," there are two other matters of interest in *The Canterbury Tales*. Both the Merchant and the Franklin are described in "The General Prologue," and each tells a tale. Since it seems fair to say that Chaucer did not intend his pilgrims to be strict types of the Seven Deadly Sins, we have in the portraits of these men good information about their position in society and their occupations.

The description of the Merchant covers lines 270 to 284 of "The

16

General Prologue." He sits high on a horse, and is well dressed. His clothing is *mottelee,* which Robinson defines as "a cloth woven with a figured design, often parti-colored" (page 657). He wears a beaver hat from Flanders and good boots. It appears the notion that clothes make the man was not unknown to the fourteenth century. There is a suggestion that the Merchant is pompous: "His resons he spak ful solempnely" (line 274), *resons* means opinions, and *solempnely* means impressively or pompously.[28] The religious connotation of *solempnely* is heightened by the next line: "Sownynge alwey th' encrees of his wynnyng," which means 'proclaiming always the increase of his profit.' This gives the impression of one who treats wealth with religious reverence.[29] The next two lines refer to his desire that the sea, and presumably international commerce, be guarded against any threats. Line 278 reads, "Wel koude he in eschaunge sheeldes selle," *sheeldes* were a French coin. Robinson's note points out that the Merchant was making a profit which "was breaking the statute which forbade anyone except the royal money changers to make a profit on exchange" (page 658), which apparently constituted illegal arbitrage. Another possibility noted by Robinson is that "Possibly Chaucer means further to imply that the Merchant took usury under the color of exchange."

The next four lines give a general description of the crafty ways of merchants, but they are clearly less severe than what Chaucer's contemporaries, Gower and Langland, said about merchants:

> This worthy man ful wel his wit bisette:
> Ther wiste no wight that he was in dette,
> So estatly was he of his governaunce
> With his bargaynes and with his chevyssaunce.
> (Lines 279-282)

Chaucer repeats *worthy* in line 283, which might indicate irony, or it may refer to his high socio-economic position. He is able to hide the fact that he is in debt. *Governaunce* is glossed as "management, care; self-control, demeanor." This continues the view that the Merchant makes a good appearance. Robinson's note to line 282 says that *bargayn* and *chevyssaunce* were "constantly used for dishonest practices . . . . sometimes a term for usury, and this implication may be intended here."[31]

The other pilgrim chosen for discussion here is the Franklin. As Robinson's note points out: "The exact social status of franklins is a matter of dispute" (page 659). In answer to the view that the Franklin is a parvenu, Robinson says,

> But Professor Gerould has collected considerable evidence that franklins were not merely men of substance, but were regarded as gentlemen, with a social position similar to that of knights, esquires, and sergeants of law. Certainly Chaucer's Franklin is described as a person of wealth and dignity.

The controversy about the Franklin's social position seems to stem in part at least from his *nouveau riche* characteristics, which would not restrict him from consideration here. As far as business dealings are concerned, the Franklin, as will be made clear, fits the purpose of this investigation.

Chaucer describes the Franklin as having a sanguine complexion, following the four humors,[32] and this is interpreted by critics as a favorable description. The *Oxford English Dictionary* says "sanguine" implies "a courageous, hopeful, and amorous disposition."[33] Furthermore, C. S. Lewis identifies sanguine temperaments as the best of the four, and calls Chaucer's Franklin ". . . a text-book case of this complexion, could give his cook a sound rating, but he had obviously a good heart."[34]

In the thirty lines devoted to the Franklin in "The General Prologue," several describe his love of food and drink. He likes wine in the morning, and his house 'snows' with food and drink. His ale is the best, and his table is always filled with fish, meat, and other food.

> To lyven in delit was evere his wone,
> For he was Epicurus owene sone,
> That heels opinioun that pleyn delit
> Was verray felicitee parfit.
> (Lines 335-338)

There may be a tinge of irony here: Epicurus was associated with

18

Chaucer's Merchant

false virtue by Boethius and St. Augustine, partly because only fragments of his philosophy were known.[35]

Chaucer devotes six lines to the legal and political duties of the Franklin. He was a member of Parliament for his county, and presided over sessions of the Justice of the Peace. He had been a knight of the shire and a sheriff. He was also a substantial landholder *(vavasour)*, and a *contour*, a word which may mean a sergeant of law, a pleader in court, or an accountant. The final meaning implies, according to Robinson, that he may have been an auditor on the shire.

We learn more about the Franklin from the Prologue to his tale. He describes himself as unlearned:

> But, sires, by cause I am a burel man,
> At my bigynnyng first I yow biseche,
> Have me excused of my rude speche.
> I lerned nevere rethorik, certeyn;
> Thyng that I speke, it moot be bare and pleyne.
> (Lines 716-720)

These lines may be intended to characterize the Franklin as a sort of Medieval Babbitt. Robinson points out, however, that this kind of "modesty prologue" was used fairly often. Later in *The Canterbury Tales*, Chaucer the pilgrim, tells the tale of "Sir Thopas," that is so bad, the Host interrupts, and Chaucer must tell another story. The Parson also says he is not able to (and presumably unwilling to) rhyme his tale. These words of the Franklin may represent humility.[36] It could also be a rhetorical device, aimed at making himself look unintelligent in order to make his point more emphatically.[37] However, the Babbitt similarity must be considered again. Of the twenty lines in his Prologue, thirteen are taken up by references to his lack of knowledge. This suggests he is a wind-bag, who cannot limit his speech.

The descriptions of the Merchant and the Franklin constitute the only direct characterizations of businessmen made by Chaucer. Within the poem there are three other topics for investigation: "The Merchant's Tale," "The Franklin's Tale," and "The Shipman's Tale." Each one fits into the general topic of love narratives; in the third, a merchant is a main character. We

20

must, however, introduce the complexities of indirectness. The merchant in "The Shipman's Tale" is devised in order to fit the storyteller's purpose, and may represent a manipulated portrait of a medieval businessman. The other two tales, while not about business, may offer valuable insights into the characters of the tellers, who are businessmen.

"The Shipman's Tale" is a fabliau of "The Lover's Gift Regained" type.[38] The wife of a rich merchant requests a 'gift' from a monk, who claims to be the merchant's cousin, and who is a friend of the family. The monk borrows the money from the merchant, gives it to the wife, and spends an amatory evening in the merchant's absence. When asked about the loan, the monk says he gave it to the wife. The merchant asks her about it, and she says she used it to pay for clothes, and is able to talk him out of considering it a debt she owes him.

It has been argued by George Lyman Kittredge,[39] Furnivall, Skeat, Tatlock and others that this tale was intended originally for the Wife of Bath. It has been suggested further that the merchant in this story should be seen in contrast to the Merchant in "The General Prologue" — perhaps the Shipman was taunting him. These interpretations see the merchant in "The Shipman's Tale" as generous to his wife's financial demands, and honest in his business dealings. The implication is that the Merchant of "The General Prologue" is unhappily married, which seems to be borne out by his tale, and that he is dishonest. The Shipman's merchant tells his wife how tough it is to succeed in business:

> We may wel make chiere and good visage,
> And dryve forth the world as it may be,
> And kepen oure estaat in pryvetee,
> Til we be deed, or elles that we pleye
> A pilgrymage, or goon out of the weye.
> (Lines 230-234)

Kittredge suggests the pilgrims must have looked at the Merchant, thinking he might have made a pilgrimage to dodge his creditors (page 173). We also see the merchant in "The Shipman's Tale" as a cuckold, who never even learns he has been cuckolded, indicating how the pilgrims needled each other.

John C. McGalliard has argued that the merchant in "The Shipman's Tale" is an honest, intelligent, generous man, and that he does not typify avarice, philistinism, or crass materialism.[40] Professor McGalliard also points out that Chaucer has given considerable attention to the medieval mercantile milieu, and that this milieu resembles that of the twentieth century businessman. The merchant, in explaining how difficult it is to succeed in business, says, "Scarsly amonges twelve tweye shul thryve" (line 228), or that less than 16.6% of businessmen prosper continually. Clifford M. Baumback, et al. in *How to Organize and Operate a Small Business* estimate that about 20% of new businesses succeed.[41] Without considering Chaucer's use of statistics, it is interesting that six centuries have not altered significantly the likelihood of success for businessmen!

*Chevyssaunce* appears several times in the tale. Professor McGalliard sees no moral overtones about this arrangement as far as the merchant is concerned. There is certainly no explicit mention of usury, and the merchant himself lends money freely to the monk — without interest. It is not clear that there is an ironic intention in the line "For he was riche and clearly out of dette" (line 376). This certainly represents a change from the three earlier writers considered in this chapter, and from the implications about the Merchant's financial dealings in "The General Prologue."

I do, however, have several doubts about the favorable characterization of the merchant in "The Shipman's Tale," recognizing the likelihood that certain lines were intended to needle the merchant. The first two lines of the tale express the same ironic point of view one finds in *Babbitt* and *Goodbye, Columbus:*

> A marchant whilom dwelled at Seint-Denys,
> That riche was, for which men helde hym wys.
> (Lines 1-2)

We also have a picture of the merchant in his *countour-hous* (line 77) counting his profits for the year with the door locked:

> Ful riche was his tresor and his hord,
> For which ful faste his countour-dore he shette;
> And eek he nolde that no man sholde hym lette

22

Of his acountes, for the meene tyme.
(Lines 84-87)

At face value, this might suggest he was, like the Merchant of
"The General Prologue," hiding the truth about his finances.
Some might see this as suggestive of the ways of a usurer. In a
general sense, it seems to parallel tax figuring (line 79 implies this
is at year's end), and the methods of a man with a spendthrift wife
(lines 10-19 note a woman's need for large sums of money). Obviously two reasons for the merchant's characterization are the tale
and the teller. As a cuckold, he may have to be something of a
stereotype. For a variety of reasons, then, this is a pretty good
merchant without any overwhelming bad characteristics. We also
have an opportunity to learn of his two business trips — to Bruges
and Paris; his borrowing and lending; his general business concerns; and his need for secrecy about his accounts:[42]

> For everemoore we moote stonde in drede
> Of hap and fortune in oure chapmanhede.
> (Lines 237-238)

The importance of "The Merchant's Tale" for our purpose is
that it sheds more light on the overall character of the Merchant.
The description of him in "The General Prologue" is short and
fairly general. In his tale he speaks. The general impression of
critics is that the tale parallels his own marriage. The husband,
January, (old husband-young wife theme) is "A worthy knyght"
(line 1246), and lives "in greet prosperitee" (line 1247). The
numerous references to wealth, the setting in Lombardy, and the
absence of military references suggest he is a poorly disguised
merchant. The old man rejects the advice of Justinus (justice or
Justinian?) and accepts the advice of Placebo (Latin for "I will
please") and marries a young girl. Damyan, a squire, falls in love
with her. January later loses his sight. May, in the garden in
which January and May make love, meets Damyan in a tree to
make love. Pluto intervenes and gives January his sight back.
Proserpine intervenes and helps May to formulate an answer:
January's new eyes did not see properly. He kisses May, and
leads her home.
This is generally regarded as one of the harshest of *The Canter-*

23

*bury Tales.* May is portrayed as deceitful, and January as an embittered cuckold. It does 'answer' the Wife of Bath's tale by showing the rich old husband's point of view.

Of most significance for our purpose is the general character of January as, I believe, avaricious. Following the view that January is somewhat autobiographical, the Merchant seems to be confessing his own folly about women. Without making a catalogue, there are numerous references to May as if she were property, e.g., "the fruyt of his tresor" (line 1270), "verray ground of his prosperitee" (line 1622), his "paradys" (line 1822). The general idea of May as heaven on earth, or of a wife as heaven on earth, and mercantile metaphors about sex and love abound.[43] Although January may have loved May in a fashion, she did not love him. Her love for Damyan seems to have been sincere. But, unlike "The Shipman's Tale" where the merchant is fairly neutral, this tale places its sympathy on the side of January. Yet, January is a foolish character for allowing himself to be treated as he has been. The villain is clearly May, with an implication that May is like Eve, considering the prominence of the garden in this story; and the merchant implies Eve was primarily to blame.

Although lust would seem to be the major sin of January,[44] I think avarice is a better choice. In "The Parson's Tale," his discussion of Avarice begins with a reference to 1 Timothy VI,10: "For covetousness is the root of all evils, and some in their eagerness to get rich have strayed from the faith and have involved themselves in many troubles." It is safe to say that both January (a knight merchant) and the Merchant have been too covetous, as Chaucer saw it. The innuendoes of "The General Prologue" are borne out. The Merchant appears cynical, and seeks self-pity, nor is there any implication that he has turned over a new leaf. Whatever the faults of the merchant in "The Shipman's Tale," he is a far happier and morally better person than the avaricious January and the Merchant.

"The Franklin's Tale" has many similarities to "The Merchant's Tale," and may be regarded as representing an answer to the Merchant.[45] Here, a husband, out of *gentilesse,* refrains from sovereignty over his wife, becoming her "servant in love, and lord in marriage" (line 793). He then goes to England to seek fame. Dorigen is very sad, but a squire, Aurelius, seeks her love.

She says she will yield when all the rocks are removed from the coast of Brittany. He gets a magician to do it; now Dorigen fears she must live up to her oath. Arveragus returns home, and tells Dorigen she must keep her word. Aurelius releases her from her oath because of her husband's *gentilesse,* and is in turn forgiven his debt to the magician for his *gentilesse.* (This shows the magician's *gentilesse.*)

Kittredge considered this tale the solution of the marriage Group. Others have seen the story as ludicrous, and devoid of *gentilesse.* For our purposes, the Franklin's overall character could be seen as improving or weakening through his tale. On the positive side, Kittredge sees lines 760-805 as "knitting up the matter" of the marriage group. The Franklin here views the marriage of Arveragus and Dorigen as "an humble, wys accord" (line 791). It combines marriage and courtly love — the best of both possible worlds, so to speak. Many critics interpret these lines as affirming Christian virtue, true love, common sense, and *gentilesse.* It is also fairly clear that these lines are a direct answer to several 'debates' on marriage, certainly to the Merchant and the Wife of Bath. The Franklin does not advocate female sovereignty as the Wife does. However, in words that may sound like part of a recent speech, he argues for sexual equality:

> Wommen, of kynde, desiren libertee,
> And nat to been constreyned as a thral;
> And so doon men, if I sooth seyen shal.
> (Lines 768-770)

In words that answer the Merchant, the Franklin refers to this equal marital relationship as "prosperitee" (lines 799, 804).[46] It is also true that "The Franklin's Tale" upholds the sanctity of marriage, and rejects the courtly love code, which is extramarital. In what must have appeared a switch to much of Chaucer's audience, Aurelius releases Dorigen from her pledge. By implication, this is one of the most moral tales, and certainly upholds virtue more than "The Shipman's Tale," and other fabliaux.[47] This interpretation of the tale raises the dignity of the Franklin considerably.

On the other hand, there is a possible interpretation which is unfavorable to the Franklin. This view holds that the Franklin does not understand *gentilesse,* and that his story does not hang together. Arveragus swears not to take mastery (lines 745 ff.) over Dorigen. This was probably unlikely, and might have been considered unmanly. Dorigen, of course, makes the foolish promise, and then fears she may have to pay up. She considers killing herself, and launches into 89 lines of *exempla* about women who would rather die than be bereft of virtue:

> I wol conclude that it is bet for me
> To sleen myself than been defouled thus.
> I wol be trewe unto Arveragus,
> Or rather sleen myself in som manere
> (Lines 1422-1425).

She continues to feel this way for three days, when Arveragus returns. (Of course, she does not kill herself.) Arveragus is upset, but tells her to fulfill her pledge, and not to tell anyone "up peyne of deeth" (line 1481). So, Dorigen goes to Aurelius, intending to pay up. It might appear that Dorigen's lengthy speech on virtue is ironic: she does not kill herself. After complaining for days, she rather meekly obeys her husband's command, suggesting their relationship was not equal. More importantly, both characters might seem devoid of *gentilesse,* the subject the Franklin is often credited with expounding.

In addition to the story itself, the manner of telling the story may involve irony. The long list of *exempla* seems overdone. Following the quotation above, in which Dorigen says she concludes, she goes on for another twenty-nine lines listing more *exempla.* The long speech on marriage praised by Kittredge and Holman may be seen as loquaciousness. Here is a small example of this quality:

> Til that the brighte sonne loste his hewe;
> For th' orisonte hath reft the sonne his lyght, —
> This is as much to seye as it was nyght!
> (Lines 1017-1019).

After he tells the resolution of the story, the Franklin asks,

"What sholde I lenger of this cas endyte?" (line 1550). This loquaciousness together with the possible lack of *gentilesse* would make the Franklin rather pompous, a characteristic he would share with the Merchant.

The four writers who have been considered in this chapter show a fairly wide variety of attitudes toward the medieval businessman. Dante, Gower, and Langland appear to concentrate on evil aspects of merchants, although these characterizations of merchants should not be taken as condemning all medieval businessmen. In Chaucer we see the stereotype of the businessman, but we also see a fuller depiction of the merchant in his milieu. Dante, Gower, and Langland referred to merchants as part of their overall purposes — the discussion of avarice and penitence. Who would be more likely to be charged with avarice than a businessman? In Chaucer, for various reasons, we see the same charges levelled at businessmen. Chaucer himself makes the charges, but so do other pilgrims. This suggests a certain rivalry among social classes at that time, which accounts in part for the general impression that the Merchant and the Franklin are *nouveau riche*. Of the three businessmen in *The Canterbury Tales,* one (the Merchant) seems to be a rather negative character, similar to the merchants in *The Divine Comedy, Confessio Amantis,* and *Piers the Plowman.* The Franklin could be interpreted in a favorable or unfavorable manner — certainly he is not all bad. His faults are not avarice and usury, but some false humility and a lack of sophistication. The merchant in "The Shipman's Tale" is interpreted by Professor McGalliard as at least not an evil person. The references to his possible miserliness seem intended to needle the Merchant and the Wife of Bath.

In concluding this chapter, I would like to knit up three general considerations: 1) the milieu of the businessman; 2) the similarities among the businessmen in the four writers considered; and 3) implications about the similarities and differences between medieval businessmen and modern businessmen.

In *The Divine Comedy* there is no clear distinction made between good businessmen and bad businessmen. Usurers are condemned, presumably for their greedy, anti-social avarice and fraud. In both Gower and Langland we get more specific information about how the evil businessmen went about being evil: they cheated in the sale of goods; they demanded excessive return on loans; and they did not attend to religious duties. Whereas Dante has no sympathy for businessmen, and does not deign to speak to one, both Gower and Langland appear to have had closer personal contact with businessmen, and give specific examples of why businessmen are fraudulent. Langland gives several examples of places to which merchants travelled. Finally, in Chaucer, we learn far more about the day to day life of the merchant. It is interesting that the brief, stock description of the Merchant in "The General Prologue" is so negative, but the merchant in "The Shipman's Tale" contrasts sharply with the Merchant. The Shipman's merchant lends without interest, but borrows at interest, which is very different from *Inferno* in which all interest appears evil. Chaucer's Merchant may be evil, but he receives a much fuller treatment than Dante's usurers. The Merchant's evils are clearly derived from moral choices, and are not the result of 'guilt by association.' This general charge in the treatment of merchants and their milieu agrees with the position of most historians. Charles Homer Haskins says the merchants were the bourgeoisie of the future, and added a fourth class to medieval society.[48] A term often heard is "the rise of the merchant class;"[49] with this rise, the evils of usury were de-emphasized, and the need for interest-bearing loans became established. There is also the implication that merchants and businessmen in general became far more numerous. If one looks for a businessman in Old English literature (to 1100), he would look in vain.

Recognizing the development of a mercantile class, we can look for similarities in the characterizations of businessmen by the four poets included here. Dante, Gower, Langland, and Chaucer's Merchant have strong similarities: businessmen are fraudulent, avaricious, and usurers. Within *The Canterbury Tales*, the Merchant and the merchant in "The Shipman's Tale" are described as secretive about finances,[50] and as *nouveau riche*. Both the Franklin and the Merchant are somewhat pompous, and *nouveau riche*. Only the Merchant is a usurer; the Shipman's merchant lends freely. The Franklin is described as generous. So we have the stock evils of businessmen, but they are not adhered to rigidly. There is no suggestion that the Franklin is a usurer, and no suggestion of pomposity in the Shipman's merchant. Indeed, his negative qualities are ascribed primarily to needle the Merchant. This shows a considerable development of the businessman as a literary figure from his absence in Old English literature and his summary condemnation in Dante.

The final consideration in this chapter is the similarities and dissimilarities of the medieval businessman and the modern businessman. In *The Worldly Philosophers*, Robert Heilbroner writes, "In the Middle Ages the Church taught that 'no Christian ought to be a merchant.'"[51] Heilbroner says that the American Pilgrims also felt gain was immoral. The evidence presented here shows that the businessman and his milieu were regarded as complex in the Middle Ages, and the moral critique of commerce was not wholly one-sided. The evils of usury were the same to Chaucer as they had been to Dante; however, as business developed, and money dealing became established, the stereotype of the businessman as evil was removed. It is also significant that Chaucer's Parson makes no mention of usury in his discussion of Avarice. He does, however, discuss the *thraldom* created by financial obligations, and accuses lords of *extorcions* in taking money from bondsmen and *underlynges*. Following this he distinguished between good merchants and bad merchants. What is at the basis of the Parson's discussion, I believe, is social mobility. Then, as now, money was a means of raising one's social status. However, those who make others slaves to money are un-Christian. Although the Parson offers no praise for businessmen, we see him affirming what one scholar called the "intelligence and energy" of social mobility "instead of being measured by social status" and "the rank of each class."[52] Along with this social mobility comes the charge of lack of appropriate sophistication, which may sound very similar to the twentieth century.

We are left with the problem of usury. Heilbroner says of the Middle Ages, "The broader notion that a general struggle for gain might actually bind together a community would have been held as little short of madness" (page 25). This must now be regarded as a vague generalization. But let us consider whether a "struggle for gain" is highly regarded in our own time. Since the "robber baron" period there have been numerous laws intended to create fairness in business practices. Interest rates, except in loansharking, are not left to the discretion of the lender. There are laws against monopolies, unfair pricing, dishonest competition, insider stock trading, bribes, and tax fraud. We are still faced with the issue of unearned profit. The "struggle for gain" has been reduced somewhat by a graduated income tax, free education, and inheritance taxes. Overall, our century faces the same moral dilemmas the thirteenth and fourteenth centuries faced. The growth of business, however, has not eliminated the need for control.

# Footnotes

[1] Paolo Milano, "Introduction," *The Portable Dante* (New York: The Viking Press, 1947), p. xlii.
Fredi Chiappelli, "Introduzione," *Dante Alighieri: Tutte Le Opere* (Milano: U. Mursia & Co., 1965), pages xvi-xvii.
[2] John D. Sinclair, "Preface," *The Divine Comedy of Dante Alighieri: Inferno* (New York: Oxford University Press, 1939), pages 10-11.
[3] Sir Philip Sidney, "The Defense of Poesy" (1595) in: *Tudor Poetry and Prose*, ed. J. William Hebel, et al. (New York: Appleton-Century-Crofts, Inc., 1953), pages 801-838.
[4] G. C. Macaulay, "Introduction," *The English Works of John Gower*, Vol. I. (London: Oxford University Press, 1969 rpt.), p. viii.
[5] Kemp Malone and Albert C. Baugh, "The Middle Ages (to 1500)" in: *A Literary History of England.* 2nd ed. (New York: Appleton-Century-Crofts, 1967).
[6] Walter W. Skeat, "Introduction," *The Vision of William Concerning Piers the Plowman In Three Parallel Texts by William Langland* (London: Oxford University Press, 1969 rpt.), p. xxvii.
[7] George Lyman Kittredge, *Chaucer and His Poetry* (Cambridge: Harvard University Press, 1915), p. 2.
[8] Sinclair, p. 19.
[9] Lines 72-73 of the canto.
[10] D. Mantovani, *Lecturae Dantis,* quoted in Sinclair, p. 222.
[11] *The Compact Edition of the Oxford English Dictionary*, ed. C. T. Onions, et al. (Oxford: Oxford University Press, 1971). Vol. II, p. 3577: Richard Brunne, *Handlyng Synne,* line 2417, calls a usurer a thief; William Langland, *Piers Plowman,* Book 14, line 175, calls usury secret.
[12] *A Latin Dictionary Founded on Andrews' Edition of Freund's Latin Dictionary,* rev. Charlton T. Lewis and Charles Short (Oxford: The Clarendon Press, 1879), p. 1947.
[13] Henry Campbell Black, *Black's Law Dictionary,* 4th ed. (St. Paul:

West Publishing Co., 1951). He distinguishes usury in modern law from usury in Old English law. In modern law, it refers to "illegal interest;" whereas in Old English law, it refers to:

> Interest of money; increase for the loan of money; a reward for the use of money. . . . The taking of any compensation whatever for the use of money (p. 1714).

Although Italy and England did not subscribe to a single legal code, this medieval view of usury seems to have been common to both.

[14]Friedrich Heer, *The Medieval World*, trans. Janet Sondheimer (New York: The New American Library, 1961), pages 80-81.

[15]Karl Witte, *Essays on Dante*, trans. C. Mable Lawrence and Philip H. Wicksteed (London, 1898), p. 7.

[16]John D. Sinclair, ed., *The Divine Comedy of Dante Alighieri: Il Purgatorio* (New York: Oxford University Press, 1939), p. 15.

[17]A. C. Baugh, p. 202.

[18]The specific Biblical references are, Achan — Joshua, VII; Ananias and Sapphira — Acts, V, 1-11; Heliodorus — 2 Machabees III.

[19]Vergil, *Aeneid*, ed. Charles Knapp (Chicago: Scott, Foresman and Company, 1923), "Vocabulary," p. 64.

[20]Pope Innocent III, "On the Misery of Man," in: *Two Views of Man*, trans. Bernard Murchland (New York, 1966), p. 38.

[21]Macaulay, p. xxi.

[22]Skeat's note concerns *auncel* in line 224, page 84:

> *Auncel,* a kind of balance, perhaps the Danish steelyard. Blount tells us, in his Law-Dictionary, that 'because there was wont to be great deceit [in its use], it was forbidden,' 23 Edw. 3, Stat. 5. Cap. 9; 34 ejusdem, cap. 5; and 8 Hen. 6, cap. 5.

[23]We also have in this passage some information about the nature of trading in the Middle Ages. Bruges was a major international market in the late Middle Ages. The remark about having to wait for profit from Prussia is interpreted by Skeat and Thomas Wright as implying that some risk attached to that trade. Wright also says that 'Prussia was then the farthest country in the interior of Europe with which a regular trade was carried on by the English merchants.'

See also Footnote 7 in Chapter 6 for a parallel with "The Merchant of Venice."

[24]Skeat's note to line 239 is, "*Usurie,* usury. 'All usury was prohibited as a sin by Canon Law;' Southey, Book of the Church, p. 187."

[25]J. R. Hulbert, "Chaucer's Pilgrims," rpt. in: *Chaucer: Modern Essays in Criticism,* ed. Edward Wagenknecht (New York: Oxford University Press, 1959), p. 23.

[26]Chaucer, Geoffrey, *The Works of Geoffrey Chaucer,* ed. F. N. Robinson. 2nd ed. (Boston: Houghton Mifflin Company, 1961), p. xix.

[27]Morton Bloomfield, *The Seven Deadly Sins* (Michigan: University of Michigan Press, 1952), p. 163.

[28]The word *solempne* had been used in line 209 to describe the Friar. According to the *Oxford English Dictionary,* the word had a religious meaning, established before *The Canterbury Tales* was written. The *O.E.D.* first entry for "solemn" says, "l. Associated or connected with religious rites or observances; performed with due ceremony and reverence; having a religious character; sacred," Vol. II, p. 2910. Chaucer apparently uses the word to create irony. ·

[29]There is at least a general similarity in these two lines to Langland's description of Avarice, who uses "the grace of gyle" (C text VII, line 213) to sell his goods. Although here it seems to be ironic rather than accusatory.

[30]Robinson goes on in his note to say that "illustrations of both fraudulent money-changing and the concealment of debts . . . were perhaps stock charges against the merchants" (p. 658). Since money-changing is mentioned specifically, I would suggest the story of Christ throwing the money-changers out of the temple (Matthew XXI, 12-13) may be applicable.

[31]The word *chevance* has been used by both Gower and Langland to describe usurers. Gower uses the word once in line 4424 of Book V within his treatment of usury discussed earlier. He uses it one other time in *Confessio Amantis* in discussing robbery: "Riht as a thief makth his chevance" (V, line 6106). Langland uses the word in his description of Avarice in B text version (B V, line 249). Skeat's note compares Langland's use of the word to Chaucer's use in describing the Merchant, and says in part:

> In an ordinance against usurers (38 Edw. III.) we find that certain persons exerted themselves to maintain usury — which kind of contract, the more subtly to deceive the people, they call *exchange* or *chevisance,* whereas it might more truly be called *mescheaunce* (wickedness), Vol. II, p. 86.

Robinson's note confirms this, and adds more historical information:

> 282 *chevysaunce,* which properly referred to borrowing and lending, or dealing for profit, was constantly used (like the word bargayn) for dishonest practices. It was sometimes a term for usury, and this implication may be intended here. Or the Merchant may have been a farmer of the revenue who failed to make honest returns to the Exchequer; or again, he may have bargained unscrupulously with the King's cred-

itors. Mr. Knott (pp. 10 ff.) shows that Richard Lyons, a London merchant of the time was charged with buying the King's obligations at a discount and then obtaining full payment of them. The same man was also prosecuted for making profits on foreign exchange (p. 658).

[32]William Flint Thrall and Addison Hibbard, *A Handbook to Literature*, rev. C. Hugh Holman (New York: The Odyssey Press, 1960): "The sanguine man has a dominance of blood, is beneficent, joyous, amorous. The choleric man is easily angered, impatient, obstinate, vengeful. The phlegmatic man is dull, pale, cowardly. The melancholic man is gluttonous, backward, unenterprising, thoughtful, sentimental, affected" (p. 230).

[33]Vol. II, p. 2636.

[34]C. S. Lewis, *The Discarded Image* (Cambridge: Cambridge University Press, 1964), p. 171.

[35]Boethius, *De Consolatione Philosophiae,* Book III, prose 2; St. Augustine, *De Civitate Dei,* Book XIX, Chapter 1.

[36]To show that the "modesty prologue" has not been abandoned by the twentieth century, here are the opening lines from Adlai Stevenson's acceptance speech for the 1952 Democratic Presidential nomination:

Mr. President, Ladies and Gentlemen of the Convention, my Fellow Citizens:

I accept your nomination — and your program.

I should have preferred to hear those words uttered by a stronger, a wiser, a better man than myself. . . .

(From — *Democratic National Convention: Official Proceedings,* 1952, pages 547-550; quoted in: A. Craig Baird, *American Public Addresses 1740-1952* (New York: McGraw Hill, 1956), p. 290.

[37]The Franklin has a personal reason for getting his message across. The tale immediately before is "The Squire's Tale." The Franklin takes a liking to the Squire, and compares him to his own son, who has bad habits, preferring possessions to virtue *(gentilesse).* This irritates the Host, who has apparently heard enough about *gentilesse.* Before telling a tale that is based on *gentilesse,* the Franklin says he will follow the Host's suggestions:

"Gladly, sire Hoost," quod he, "I wole obeye
Unto your wyl; now herkneth what I seye.
I wol yow nat contrarien in no wyse
As fer as that my wittes wol suffyse.
I prey to God that it may plesen yow;
Thanne woot I wel that it is good ynow."
(Lines 703-708)

[38]Robinson's note refers to John Webster Spargo, "The Shipman's

Tale," in: W. F. Bryan and Germaine Dempster, eds., *Sources and Analogues of Chaucer's Canterbury Tales* (Chicago: University of Chicago Press, 1941).

[39]Kittredge, p. 170. See also Robinson's note, p. 732.

[40]John C. McGalliard, "Characterization in Chaucer's *Shipman's Tale*," *Philological Quarterly*, LIV, No. 1 (Winter, 1975), 1-18.

[41]Clifford M. Baumback, Kenneth Lawyer, and Pearce C. Kelley, *How to Organize and Operate a Small Business*, 5th ed. (Englewood Cliffs: Prentice-Hall, Inc., 1973): "In normal times more than 1,000 new concerns open their doors each business day, and almost as many (approximately 800) close" (p. 22).

[42]The wife berates him for spending so long counting his money in secret (lines 214-223), which may be the reason he feels the need for secrecy. In reference to the view that "The Shipman's Tale" was intended as the Wife of Bath's second tale, she says in the prologue to her tale:

> But tel me this: why hydestow, with sorwe,
> The keyes of thy cheste awey fro me?
> It is my good as wel as thyn, pardee!
> (Lines 308-310)

In "The Shipman's Tale," the merchant acts similarly, but later forgives her the debt — a solution agreeable to the Wife of Bath, and to many women who shop in Bloomingdale's.

[43]For wedlock is so esy and so clene,
That in this world it is a paradys.
(Lines 1264-1265)
That wyf is mannes helpe and his confort,
His paradys terrestre, and his disport.
(Lines 1331-1332)
A wife may be ". . . a wastour of thy good"
(Line 1535)
Ther may no man han parfite blisses two, —
This is to seye, in erthe and eek in hevene.
(Lines 1638-1639)
That I shal have myn hevene in erthe heere.
For sith that verray hevene is boght so deere
With tribulacion and greet penaunce
(Lines 1647-1649)
And whan he wolde paye his wyf hir dette
(Line 2048)
Where money is concerned:
"For she wol clayme half part al hir lyf"
(Line 1300)

34

For a parallel to the Wife of Bath, see Footnote 42.

[44]There is a link between "The Merchant's Tale" and "The Parson's Tale" noted by Robinson. January says a man can do no sin with his own wife (lines 1839 ff.), but the Parson rejects this view (line 859).

[45]C. Hugh Holman, "Courtly Love in the Merchant's and the Franklin's Tales," rpt. in: *Chaucer: Modern Essays in Criticism,* ed. Edward Wagenknecht (New York: Oxford University Press, 1959), pages 240-250. Holman points out that each has three main characters: husband-knight, wife, squire. In each, the squire falls in love with the wife, and the husband is "away" temporarily (blind in "The Merchant's Tale"). There are supernatural events, a garden, and a reconciliation of husband and wife. Note the similarities to "The Shipman's Tale."

[46]Cf., "The Merchant's Tale," lines 1247, 1622, and 2070.

[47]I will not press this point, but Aurelius, in pining for Dorigen, is compared to Echo dying for love of Narcissus (lines 951-952). Robinson feels Chaucer is following Ovid. Chaucer probably knew Gower's version of the Echo story. Considering that the courtly love code is not exalted in "The Franklin's Tale," there is at least a general similarity in the use of the Echo story by Gower and Chaucer. I would not press an interpretation that sees Aurelius as a love usurer, but both Gower and Chaucer appear wary of the courtly love code.

[48]Charles Homer Haskins, *The Renaissance of the Twelfth Century* (Cambridge: Harvard University Press, 1953), p. 62.

[49]A. R. Meyers, *England in the Late Middle Ages (1307-1536)* (Middlesex, England: Penguin Books Ltd., 1952).

[50]McGalliard sees this as perfectly normal in "The Shipman's Tale."

[51]Robert L. Heilbroner, *The Worldly Philosophers.* 4th ed. (New York: Simon and Schuster, 1972), pages 22-23.

[52]H. Pirenne, *Medieval Cities* (Princeton: Princeton University Press, 1925), pages 127-128.

# CHAPTER THREE

## The Sixteenth and Seventeenth Centuries:
## Christopher Marlow, William Shakespeare, John Milton

The businessman is not a major figure in English literature in the sixteenth and seventeenth centuries. The most obvious works are Shakespeare's "The Merchant of Venice," and a somewhat similar play, Marlowe's "The Jew of Malta." Each concern a Jewish merchant, and his being Jewish is more significant than his being a merchant. A general similarity with medieval literature is apparent. Usury is an important theme in "The Merchant of Venice," a source of which is the Middle English poem *Cursor Mundi*. There is also a stock condemnation of merchants. John Milton's prose is concerned primarily with ecclesiastical and civil liberty. I was able to find three references to business in one of his latest prose works, "The Ready and Easy Way to Establish a Free Commonwealth."

"The Merchant of Venice" (1596) was written shortly after "The Jew of Malta" (1588-92). Each play reflects a strongly negative view of Jews. "The Jew of Malta" has not been, to my knowledge, performed often in recent years. As far as Shylock is concerned, there has been a tradition, beginning in 1841 according to Craig, of humanizing Shylock.[1] In reference to Shylock's famous lines which begin "Hath not a Jew eyes?" (III, i, 60 ff), Craig says, "The appeal cannot but attract sympathy to

Shylock."[2] Shakespeare's and Marlowe's attitudes toward Jews are not the primary investigation of this chapter, but anti-Semitism is clearly linked to Barabas's and Shylock's characters. In "The Merchant of Venice," Bassanio and Antonio are merchants, as is Shylock. There is a clear distinction among them: Bassanio and Antonio are good, Christian merchants, and Shylock is an evil, Jewish merchant. It should be remembered that "The Merchant of Venice" is a comedy, although the grimmest comedy Shakespeare wrote. It appears that Shylock does not reform himself. I would suggest, in contrast to the sentimentalized view of Shylock, that Shakespeare had almost no sympathy for him, and that Shylock's complete failure to attain his desires makes him an arch-buffoon. He loses his wealth and his daughter, who becomes a Christian, rejecting her father; and Shylock must become Christian. He also loses his bond against Antonio, and is humiliated by Portia's courtroom cleverness.

Barabas in "The Jew of Malta" is, if possible, a more evil character than Shylock. After Turks have captured the town, Barabas, who has befriended them, agrees to help the Christians by devising a plot to burn the Turkish leaders. The Christians agree, but let Barabas fall into his own trap. The Christians then capture the Turks. Barabas is described throughout as a thoroughly greedy, devious person. A standard view of "The Jew of Malta" is that its dramatic force weakens after the second act, partly because the anti-Semitism becomes intense. T. S. Eliot regarded the play as a 'savage farce.' By comparison to Barabas, Shylock has more human feeling.

It is important to consider the overall nature of these plays, and the extent to which anti-Semitism carries over into remarks about Barabas and Shylock as businessmen. So strong has been the impression of Shylock that it remains in current usage a common noun:

> shylock . . . n. Also Shylock. A heartless, exacting creditor. After Shylock, the ruthless usurer in Shakespeare's *Merchant of Venice* (1595).[3]

Shylock is made even more evil by contrast to the theme of Christian mercy, expounded by Portia in the famous speech beginning

"The quality of mercy is not strain'd" (IV, i, 184 ff.). Shylock has no mercy. Hardin Craig has suggested that Barabas' tragic fate is the result of "guilt and is a function of character and conscience," which makes Barabas a tragic "hero," but a reprehensible one.

Both Shylock and Barabas can be viewed as false within their own religion. After Barabas's goods are confiscated to give to the Turks, three Jews console him, asking him to be patient, and to remember Job. His reply:

> What tell you me of Job? . . .
> I had at home, and in mine argosy
> . . .
> As much as would have bought his
>     beasts and him
> (I, ii).

In I, iii, Antonio discusses the loan with Shylock, who says he cannot raise the money instantly. Antonio breaks in that he neither lends nor borrows at interest, but will break the custom for Bassanio. Shylock begins to tell the story of Jacob and Laban's sheep (Genesis, XXX, 25-33). Antonio cuts him off, and says, "And what of him? did he take interest?" Shylock goes on at some length telling the story to suggest that Jacob gained interest. Antonio replies that the sheep Jacob got were by God's design, and should not be cited to justify Shylock's usury. Antonio's anger flares again, and he addresses Bassanio:

> The devil can cite Scripture for his purpose.
> An evil soul producing holy witness
> Is like a villain with a smiling cheek,
> A goodly apple rotten at the heart:
> O, what a goodly outside falsehood hath!
> (I, iii, 99-103).

Shylock, then, is a Jew, who is also evil. Barabas rejects the admonitions of the three Jews. Although anti-Semitism is usually assumed to be at the root of the creation of Shylock and Barabas, they are portrayed as evil in opposition to Jewish standards.[4]

Shylock

Usury is a charge against Shylock and Barabas. Following the discussion between Shylock and Antonio noted above, Shylock makes open reference to his usury.[5] Several lines on, Shylock proposes the pound of flesh as the penalty for not paying the sum. This grotesque bond is itself a form of usury, and expresses Shakespeare's feelings about the evil power a usurious money-lender holds over the borrower. After learning that one of Antonio's ships has been wrecked, Shylock's vengeful nature appears,

> . . . let him look to his bond:
> he was wont to call me usurer;
> let him look to his bond: he was
> wont to lend money for a Christian
> courtesy; let him look to his bond.
> (III, i, 49-52).

Here he mocks money lending without interest, and shows his anger at being called a usurer. He derives a cruel joy from feeling he will collect his grotesque interest. In the court scene, several characters try to talk Shylock out of taking Antonio's flesh. Portia says no power can alter an established decree, and is praised by Shylock. She asks if he intends to have a surgeon stop the bleeding, and Shylock answers that that is not in the bond. But, Portia points out, the bond does not allow for a drop of blood. Since Shylock refused the principal, the bond is forfeited. In this comedy, Shylock's monstrous cruelty is foiled. In Craig's introduction, he notes a version of this story in *Cursor Mundi,* and comments on the tradition of such bonds:

> . . . the theme of the bond and the pound of flesh, an old widely distributed story resting ultimately on the provisions of Roman law which allowed creditors power over the lives and limbs of their debtors.[6]

Craig goes on to say that although interest-taking has become more acceptable in this century, it ". . . was then to a greater degree, a frightful weapon in the hands of the lawless and mercenary."[7]

Usury is not a major theme in "The Jew of Malta," but Barabas confesses his involvement:

> Then after that was I an usurer,
> And with extorting, cozening, forfeiting,
> And tricks belonging unto brokery,
> I filled the jails with bankrupts in a year,
> And with young orphans planted hospitals,
> And every moon made some or other mad,
> And now and then one hang himself
>     for grief,
> Pinning upon his breast a long great scroll
> How I with interest tormented him.
> But mark how I am blest for
>     plaguing them;
> I have as much coin as will buy the town.
> (II, iii).

In justifying usury, Barabas makes himself appear particularly cruel. This may be a stock charge, since Barabas does not engage in interest taking during the play.

In addition to usury, there are other attitudes about merchants found in the two plays. The lines about usury and brokery quoted above are part of a discussion Barabas has with Ithamore, a slave. Barabas's attitude about business is introduced in these lines:

> Hast thou no trade? then listen to my words,
> And I will teach thee that shall stick
>     by thee:
> First be thou void of these affections,
> Compassion, love, vain hope, and
>     heartless fear,
> Be moved at nothing, see thou pity none,
> But to thyself smile when the
>     Christians moan.

When the two speeches are put together, there is an implication that tradesmen are honest workers, but merchants are evil in the very nature of their work. The view that gaining wealth is sinful is

42

expressed by both Ferneze, the Governor of Malta, and the First
Knight in Act I, scene ii:

> *1st Knight:* From naught at first
>   thou com'st to little wealth,
> From little unto more, from more to most:
> If your first curse fall heavy on thy head,
> And make thee poor and scorned of all
>   the world,
> 'Tis not our fault, but thy inherent sin . . . .
> *Fern:* Excess of wealth is cause of covetousness:
> And covetousness, O, 'tis a monstrous sin.

The sinfulness of greed is expressed in human terms, as it was in
the Medieval works treated earlier. Immediately preceding the
lines quoted above, Ferneze answers Barabas's charge that his
goods are being stolen.

> *Fern:* No, Jew, we take particularly thine
> To save the ruin of a multitude:
> And better one want for the common good
> Than many perish for a private man.

The nature of Barabas' sin is anti-social; there is no love for other
men in his actions and desires.

Shakespeare also regards usury as an imbalance within the social order. Shylock first appears in Act I, scene iii, three hundred
thirty-two lines after the opening of the play. Shakespeare has
already set the tone for the audience's understanding of usury.
The friendship of Antonio for Bassanio, and the love of Bassanio
for Portia appear early. Bassanio's need for credit is linked to
love and friendship. Shylock's usury appears particularly evil
since he shows no regard for love and friendship. Act I, scene ii
opens with Portia and Nerissa talking.

> *Nerissa:* . . . they are sick that
> surfeit with too much as they that
> starve with nothing. It is no
> mean happiness therefore, to be
> seated in the mean . . .
> (I, ii, 6-9)

Following these themes, Shylock's greed appears inhuman. Shakespeare's comedies reduce characters who exhibit an imbalance in their personalities to normalcy. Shylock's failure to attain this social harmony makes him grotesque.

E. M. W. Tillyard in *The Elizabethan World Picture* has studied the idea of order, cosmic and earthly in the age of Shakespeare, Donne, and Milton. He refers three times to lines spoken by Lorenzo, Jessica's lover:

> Sit, Jessica. Look how the floor of heaven
> Is thick inlaid with patines of bright gold:
> There's not the smallest orb which
> thou behold'st
> But in his motion like an angel sings,
> Still quiring to the young-eyed cherubins;
> Such harmony is in immortal souls;
> But whilst this muddy vesture of decay
> Doth grossly close it in, we cannot hear it.
> (V, i, 58-65).

These lines draw a sharp distinction between the world as we know it, and man's prelapsarian state. Many other lines in the play follow this theme.

> *Ant.* I hold the world but as the
> world, Gratiano;
> A stage where every man must play a part,
> And mine a sad one.
> (I, i, 77-79).

The first line of the play is Antonio's "In sooth, I know not why I am so sad." Portia's first line is, "By my troth, Nerissa, my little body is aweary of this great world" (I, ii, 1). In this context, usury appears drab and bleak,[8] and an offense to social harmony and cosmic order.

Since usury and covetousness were regarded as sinful excesses to Shakespeare and Marlowe, the question remains, was business ever regarded as good to these poets? Bassanio and Antonio are merchants, and Bassanio shows his spiritual insight by choosing the correct casket of the three — gold, silver, *lead* — and thereby winning Portia. "So may the outward shows be least themselves: / The world is still deceived with ornament" (III, ii, 73-74). Portia expresses her love with an interesting business analogy:

> That only to stand high in your account,
> I might in virtues, beauties, livings, friends,
> Exceed account . . .
> (III, ii, 157-159).

It is Antonio, for love of Bassanio, who agrees to accept Shylock's bond. Among others, the Duke pleads with Shylock to show mercy:

> But, touch'd with human gentleness and love,
> Forgive a moiety of the principal;
> Glancing an eye of pity on his losses,
> That have of late so huddled on his back,
> Enow to press a royal merchant down
> And pluck commisseration of his state . . .
> (IV, i, 25-30).

This makes Shylock evil among merchants, and devoid of mercy.

Certainly the overall image of merchants in these two plays is a darkly evil one. Despite Antonio and Bassanio, Shylock's evil is overpowering. Both Barabas and Shylock are devoid of mercy or love, full of covetousness, and openly usurious. They are the main characters, and whatever interpretations may soften their cruelty, they remain, I think, the most evil businessmen in English literature. Compared to the references to businessmen in medieval literature, Barabas and Shylock are more fully developed, and more thoroughly evil. The medieval poets studied in the previous chapter were more sympathetic to sinfulness. Marlowe, even more than Shakespeare, exhibits every detail of Barabas's evil. The later morality plays resembled this, but Marlowe's poetic skill and fuller characterization surpass the effect in any medieval play I know. T. S. Eliot's remark is understandable, given the relentlessly evil nature of Barabas. Similarly, attempts to humanize Shylock, while partially a reaction against anti-

Semitism, express concern about Shylock's unmitigated cruelty. The image of the businessman in literature became grimmer through these two plays.

Business and the businessman was not an important topic in John Milton's vast output of poetry and prose. I have been able to find only three rather general references in "The Ready and Easy Way to Establish a Free Commonwealth," which appeared in 1660, two years after Cromwell's death, and is a strong appeal not to return the Stewarts to power. The commonwealth was conceived as anathema to kingship, challenging political, religious, and philosophical defenses of government. Ecclesiastical liberty is a primary consideration; civil liberty a concomitant. Milton's work challenges all human authority by redefining in Puritan fashion man's relationship with God.

In "The Ready and Easy Way," Milton argues for "a general council of ablest men," among whose responsibilities is to "treat of commerce."[9] The second reference argues that a free commonwealth would be more equitable than a kingdom.

> I say again, this way lies free and smooth before us, is not tangled with inconveniences, invents no new encumbrances, requires no perilous, no injurious alteration of circumscription of men's lands and properties; secure, that in this commonwealth, temporal and spiritual lords removed, no man or number of men can attain to such wealth or vast possession as will need the hedge of an agrarian law (never successful, but the cause rather of sedition, save only where it began seasonably with first possession) to confine them from endangering our public liberty.[10]

This charges that inherited authority allowed the accumulation of wealth. Such an accumulation endangers liberty, but would not occur in a free commonwealth.

The final reference is contained in this excerpt from one sentence:

> But if the people be so affected as to prostitute religion and liberty to the vain and groundless apprehension

that nothing but kingship can restore trade — not remembering the frequent plagues and pestilences that then wasted this city, such as through God's mercy we never have felt since, and that trade flourishes nowhere more than in the free commonwealths of Italy, Germany, and the Low Countries, before their eyes at this day (yet if trade be grown so craving and importunate through the profuse living of tradesmen that nothing can support it but the luxurious expenses of a nation upon trifles or superfluities; so as if the people generally should betake themselves to frugality, it might prove a dangerous matter, lest tradesmen should mutiny for want of trading, and that therefore we must forego and set to sale religion, liberty, honor, safety, all concernments divine or human, to keep up trading) — if, lastly, after all this light among us, the same reason shall pass for current to put our necks again under kingship . . . our condition is not sound, but rotten . . . and will bring us soon . . . to those calamities which attend always and unavoidably on luxury . . .

Milton argues that God has shown favor to the commonwealth by suspending the plague, which had not occurred since 1625 — thirty-five years earlier. He also claims that trade has done better in free commonwealths than in kingdoms, but considers the possibility that businessmen encourage superficial desires.

The three Milton passages cited argue for free commonwealths, and presumably, free trade — at least free of royal control. He also argues that wealth is distributed more equitably in commonwealths than in kingdoms. However, there is a strongly negative reservation about businessmen in the third paragraph.

The three works treated in this chapter present a cheerless image of the businessman. Milton's advocacy of (comparatively) free trade, and Shakespeare's sympathetic treatment of Bassanio and Antonio do not overcome the characterizations of businessmen in these works. Barbaras's relentless drive to self-destruction receives no sympathy from Marlowe.

# Footnotes

[1] William Shakespeare, *Complete Works*, ed. Hardin Craig (Chicago: Scott, Foresman and Co., 1961), p. 505.

[2] *Ibid.*, p. 517.

[3] William Morris, ed., *The American Heritage Dictionary* (Boston: American Heritage Publishing Co., Inc., 1971), p. 1201.

[4] This conclusion must be qualified somewhat. There is a general sense in which Shylock and Barabas show disrespect for the Old Testament, but there are also anti-Jewish ideas and passages. Barabas considers becoming a Christian, and confesses,

> I have been zealous in the Jewish faith,
> Hard-hearted to the poor, a covetous wretch,
> That would for lucre's sake have sold my soul.
> (IV, i)

Jessica shows strong opposition to her father's convictions:

> Alack, what heinous sin is it in me
> To be ashamed to be my father's child!
> But though I am a daughter to his blood,
> I am not to his manners. O Lorenzo,
> If thou keep promise, I shall end this strife,
> Become a Christian and thy loving wife.
> (II, iii, 16-21)

Later, Lorenzo comments, "If e'er the Jew her father come to heaven, / It will be for his gentle daughter's sake" (II, iv, 34-5).

[5] I, iii, lines 109, 142.

[6] Craig, p. 503.

[7] *Ibid.*

[8] The tone in "The Merchant of Venice" is not unlike that in Gerard Manly Hopkins' "God's Grandeur," reproduced here from Oscar Williams, ed., *Major British Poets* (New York: The New American Library, 1963):

> The world is charged with the grandeur of God.
> It will flame out, like shining from shook foil;
> It gathers to a greatness, like the ooze of oil
> Crushed. Why do men then now not reck his rod?
> Generations have trod, have trod, have trod;
> And all is seared with trade; bleared,
>     smeared with toil;
> And wears man's smudge and shares man's
>     smell: the soil

Is bare now, nor can foot feel, being shod.

And for all this, nature is never spent;
  There lives the dearest freshness deep down
    things;
  And though the last lights off the black
    West went
  Oh, morning, at the brown brink eastward,
    springs —
Because the Holy Ghost over the bent
  World broods with warm breast and with ah!
    bright wings.

[9]John Milton, *Complete Poems and Major Prose,* ed. Merritt Y. Hughes (New York: The Odyssey Press, 1957), p. 888.

[10]*Ibid.,* p. 892.

[11]*Ibid.,* p. 898.

# CHAPTER FOUR


**The Eighteenth Century:**
**Addison and Steele, Jonathan Swift,**
**Oliver Goldsmith, Adam Smith, and Edmund Burke**


The eighteenth century in England saw two major devel-
opments of interest to this work. First, following the Glorious
Revolution of 1688, there was a gradual ascendancy of the middle
class. Second, it observed the French Revolution (1789), and
reacted to it. These two movements were very important for the
development of British free enterprise, and for the British attitude
toward wealth and its attainment. What is perhaps most significant about the writers selected for this chapter is that Alexander
Pope, Samuel Johnson, John Dryden, Samuel Richardson, and
Henry Fielding have not been included. Although references to
business and businessmen may appear in their writings, such references are not significant themes. In fact, of the six writers
listed, only the first four are commonly considered "literary"
men. This chapter will not attempt a lengthy analysis of the economic and political ideas of Smith and Burke. I was also unable to
find a significant body of work from Addison and Steele, Swift,
and Goldsmith, which characterizes the businessman, which is in
itself significant. The fact that a business novel does not appear
among works known to me shows that the businessman was not a
major character in eighteenth century English literature. A thor-
ough study of eighteenth century English literature may reveal

other works worthy of consideration, but such an exhaustive search has not been within the scope of this book.

Joseph Addison (1672-1719) and Richard Steele (1672-1729) are two of the best known short-essayists in English, and formed what remains probably the most celebrated literary partnership in English literature. They collaborated on *The Tatler,* a literary periodical (1709-1711), and *The Spectator* (1711-1712).

In *The Spectator* No. 69 (Saturday, May 19, 1711), Addison gives a laudatory view of trade and merchants:

> . . . there are not more useful Members in a Commonwealth than Merchants. They knit Mankind together in a mutual intercourse of good offices, distribute the Gifts of Nature, find Work for the Poor, and Wealth to the Rich, and Magnificence to the Great. . . .
>
> Trade, without enlarging the *British* Territories, has given us a kind of additional Empire: It has multiplied the Number of the Rich, made our Landed Estates infinitely more Valuable than they were formerly, and added to them an Accession of other Estates as valuable as the Lands themselves.[1]

There is a strong national pride evident here, as well as Whiggism. The setting of this essay is the Royal Exchange, where Addison feels impressed by the mixture of nationalities, and reflects on the numerous imports, which England could not enjoy without trade.

Richard Steele in *The Spectator* No. 2 (Friday, March 2, 1710-1711) describes a fictional person, Sir Andrew Freeport, who belongs to a fictional club, the "Spectator Club." Freeport is a merchant, and receives more laudatory treatment ". . . a Merchant of great Eminence . . . . A person of indefatigable Industry, strong Reason, and great Experience. His Notions of Trade are noble and generous." Sir Andrew is a new man of power, as opposed to aristocrats (old men of power), and he promises economic individualism for himself and others. This is a middle class sentiment.

Jonathan Swift (1667-1745), an Irish-born clergyman, is the greatest satirist in English literature. Unfortunately, business enterprise is not treated in *Gulliver's Travels*. If it were, it probably would have appeared in Part III "A Voyage to Laputa," in which he satirizes science by imagining Laputan scientists extracting sunbeams from cucumbers, reducing human excrement to its original food, and building houses by beginning at the roof and working downwards to the foundation.[3]

In 1724, Swift began a campaign to boycott copper coins, which William Wood — by royal patent — was to mint in England and introduce into Ireland. Swift wrote several poems on the matter, and four letters, distributed as leaflets. In these letters he took the guise of the Drapier. The first two were aimed primarily at the middle class, and he wrote as tradesmen talked, and explained the potential economic harm in everyday terms: ". . . the shopkeeper or victualer, or any other tradesman, has no more to do, than to demand ten times the price of his goods, if it is to be paid in Wood's money."[4] The ultimate outcome, Swift asserts, would be grave for all but "the gentlemen of estates:"

> But when the squire turns farmer and merchant him-
> self, all the good money he gets from abroad, he will
> hoard up to send for England, and keep some poor
> tailor or weaver, and the like, in his own house, who
> will be glad to get bread at any rate.[5]

Swift's poems on the subject concentrate more on personal ridicule of Wood, a style of argument which was more respectable in the eighteenth century than it is in the twentieth. In "Whitshed's Motto on His Coach," Swift describes a wealthy landowner: "They swear I am so kind and glad, / I hug them till I squeeze their Blood" (lines 9-10).[6] There remains some question as to whether Wood's coins were bad. Sir Isaac Newton, the Master of the Mint, said the coins were good. Swift's main purpose, however, was to stir Irish nationalism, and he succeeded. The guise of the Drapier allowed Swift to appeal to the middle class, and by his understatement and irony, he also appealed to nobility: ". . . as far as a tradesman can be thought capable of explaining . . ." This mere tradesman showed a good knowledge of Bacon, Old English law, economics, and Irish history.

Beyond the national boycott Swift aroused, he was a significant force in the history of Irish nationalism, and became a serious challenge to Robert Walpole (Whig Prime Minister 1721-1742). Both George I and Walpole were ridiculed by scatological humor and satire in Swift's works.

Swift portrayed wealthy estate owners and English government officials in a bad light. He also sympathized with and took the role of middle class merchants. By contrast, Addison and Steele portrayed the merchant as classless: he gives work to the poor, and wealth to the rich. Only thirteen years separate Addison and Steele from Swift, but in Swift, class divisions and economic conflict appear.

Oliver Goldsmith (1730-1774) is often regarded as having written the best novel, *The Vicar of Wakefield* (1766), the best play, ''She Stoops to Conquer'' (1771), and the best poem, ''The Deserted Village'' (1770) of his time. In the forty-six years that transpired between *The Drapier's Letters* and ''The Deserted Village,'' the Industrial Revolution had moved forward considerably. The developing middle class became richer. As towns and factories grew, villages became almost deserted. The last twenty-five years of the eighteenth century were severe, and this continued for the first quarter of the nineteenth century.

In ''The Deserted Village,'' Goldsmith recalls, as narrator, his own youth in a rural village. He was born and reared in County Longford, Ireland. His father, an Anglican priest, is idealized in the poem (lines 137 ff.). The first thirty-five lines recall the idyllic pleasures of his youth:

> Sweet Auburn! loveliest village of the plain,
> Where health and plenty cheer'd the labouring swain,
> Where smiling spring its earliest visit paid,
> And parting summer's ling'ring blooms delay'd,
> Dear lovely bowers of innocence and ease,
> Seats of my youth, when every sport could please,
> How often have I loiter'd o'er thy green,
> Where humble happiness endear'd each scene!
> (Lines 1-8)[7]

This verse paragraph comes to a saddening conclusion: ''These were thy charms — But all these charms are fled'' (Line 34). The reason for the change is first hinted at: "Amidst thy bowers the tyrant's hand is seen" (Line 37). A few lines farther on, Goldsmith takes aim at the cause of the problem:

> Ill fares the land, to hast'ning ills a prey,
> Where wealth accumulates, and men decay;[8]
> Princes and lords may flourish, or may fade;
> A breath can make them, as a breath has made;
> But a bold peasantry, their country's pride,
> When once destroy'd, can never be supply'd.
>
> A time there was, ere England's griefs began,
> When every rood of ground maintain'd its man;
> For him light labour spread her wholesome store,
> Just gave what life requir'd, but gave no more:
> His best companions, innocence and health;
> And his best riches, ignorance of wealth.
>
> But times are altered; trade's unfeeling train
> Usurp the land and dispossess the swain;
> Along the lawn, where scatter'd hamlets rose,
> Unwieldy wealth, and cumb'rous pomp repose;
> And every want to opulence ally'd,
> And every pang that folly pays to pride.
> (Lines 51-68)

Wealth is mentioned three times and trade once. The Industrial Revolution underlies the problems of the village, but Goldsmith is contrasting time-honored, Christian virtues with the new un-Christian desires of the rising middle-class industrialists.

Maintaining the humble perspective of a villager, he spells out the corruption of the new set of values:

> . . . The man of wealth and pride,
> Takes up a space that many poor supply'd;
> Space for his lake, his park's extended bounds,
> Space for his horses, equipage, and hounds;
> The robe that wraps his limbs in silken sloth,
> Has robb'd the neighbouring field of half their
>    growth;
> His seat, where solitary sports are seen,

55

Indignant spurns the cottage from the green;
Around the world each needful product flies,
For all the luxuries the world supplies.[9]
While thus the land adorn'd for pleasure, all
In barren splendor feebly waits the fall.
(Lines 275-286)

This is the opposite of the favorable view of the businessman found in Addison and Steele; and, whereas Swift chose the guise of a drapier, Goldsmith remains the humble villager, opposed to all the man of wealth stands for.

Goldsmith goes on to consider the plight of the peasant who must leave the village. He may bring his stock to open fields — "Those fenceless fields the sons of wealth divide, / And even the bare-worn common is deny'd" (lines 307-308). He may go to the city —

To see ten thousand baneful arts combin'd
To pamper luxury, and thin mankind;[9]
To see these joys the sons of pleasure know,
Extorted from his fellow-creature's woe.
(Lines 311-314)

As hard as Goldsmith is on urban businessmen, his main concern is the damage that has been done to virtue:

Even now the devastation is begun,
And half the business of destruction done;
Even now, methinks, as pond'ring here I stand,
I see the rural virtues leave the land.
(Lines 395-398)

Although a close analysis of Adam Smith's work is not intended here, some perspective may be gained on Smith by contrast to Goldsmith. "The Deserted Village" makes no attempt to challenge an economic system. It is set in human terms, and herein lies its power. It is this perspective which many historical economists lack. Robert Heilbroner in *The Worldly Philosophers* discusses the economic progress through specialization explained in *The Wealth of Nations:*

> But if we view the matter in its historical perspective, if we compare the lot of the workingman in eighteenth-century England to his predecessor a century or two before, it is clear that mean as his existence was, it constituted a considerable advance.[10]

This "perspective" might be correct if one merely counts material possessions. However, such a perspective belittles human sufferings.

It can also be claimed that "The Deserted Village" falls into a pattern which Smith helped develop. *The Wealth of Nations* appeared six years after Goldsmith's poem, but *The Theory of Moral Sentiments* (1759) appeared eleven years earlier. Following such philosophers as Hume and Locke, Smith considered how men may enter into the passions of other men. Thus, experience is essential to the development of morality. This veers from the conception of an inborn moral sense, and raises one's fellow-man, as long as he is worthy of approval, to a great dignity. This view of morality is also a departure from orthodox Calvinism. One of the pillars of *laissez-faire* in Smith's view is sympathy for one's fellow-man:

> How selfish soever man may be supposed, there are evidently some principles in his nature which interest him in the fortune of others, and render their happiness necessary to him, though he derives nothing from it except the pleasure of seeing it.[11]

Contained in both *The Wealth of Nations* and *The Theory of Moral Sentiments* is a justification of the accumulation of wealth. The individual represents to other individuals in his society a source of morality — through experience and observation. Both privacy and private property accrued to the individual. Before Smith, both Calvin and the American Puritans had praised the profit motive. It was Smith's belief that the happiness of other men is important to each individual. (This is a part of Smith's philosophy which is not treated adequately in *The Wordly Philosophers.*) In contrast to Smith's approval of the profit motive, and out of an overindulgent sympathy for the peasants, Goldsmith views the profit motive as destructive of morality.

Although this thesis cannot presume to be a final arbiter, the doubtfulness of Smith's belief that men are concerned with the happiness of others is demonstrated in the Industrial Revolution, and in such works as "The Deserted Village."

Edmund Burke (1729-1797) has been called the Father of English Conservatism. In *Reflections on the Revolution in France,* he contrasted England to France, and made a powerful argument for maintaining English institutions. Change in English history has been progressive, and has avoided a full-scale French-style revolution. His ideas were very influential, particularly with William Wordsworth and Samuel Taylor Coleridge. Burke considers the threat to society if trade and manufacturing should be destroyed through revolution:

> Where trade and manufacturers are wanting to a people and the spirit of nobility and religion remains, sentiment supplies, and not always ill supplies, their place; but if commerce and the arts should be lost in an experiment to try how well a state may stand without these old fundamental principles, what sort of a thing must be a nation of gross, stupid, ferocious, and, at the same time, poor and sordid barbarians, destitute of religion, honor, or manly pride, possessing nothing at present and hoping for nothing hereafter?[12]

Burke takes a cautious stance. He upholds the institutions of trade and manufacturing as better than the destruction of these institutions in a society without the "sentiment" to replace them. This expresses a less optimistic view of the goodness of human motives than that found in Smith. Writing twenty years after Goldsmith in "The Deserted Village," he is considerably more favorable toward trade and manufacturing. Burke's perspective, however, is national, whereas Goldsmith's was personal.

Although the number of literary works treated in this chapter has been small, an attempt has been made to place these works into historical perspective. Furthermore, the absence of more literature about businessmen is significant. Addison and Steele, Smith, and Burke dealt with the businessman from a national and philosophical point of view. By contrast, Goldsmith viewed the businessman as a Philistine, who was destroying time-honored virtues. His point of view was that of the small farmer, whose life was thrown into turmoil by the Industrial Revolution. George Crabbe also upheld rural life in opposition to industrialization in "The Village" (1783). Swift's treatment of the businessman is the most complex. Taking the guise of a drapier, he sided with the Irish merchants, and succeeded in stimulating united opposition to English monetary policies. The four *Drapier's Letters* were intended to appeal to the middle class (first and second), nobility (third), and the common people (fourth). It is significant that he chose the guise of a man who had ". . . a pretty good shop of Irish stuffs and silks." There are two other short poems by Swift which are light verse (or occasional poems), and which poke fun at bankers:

> A baited Banker thus desponds,
> From his own Hand foresees his Fall,
> They have his Soul who have his Bonds.[13]

The works considered here illuminate major ideas found in the work of Adam Smith. Goldsmith represents a reaction against the moral and economic assumptions of Smith. The business and economics student may gain from this discussion an appreciation of what Smith's ideas meant for farmers and villagers. The point of view expressed by Goldsmith became far more pronounced in the nineteenth century in such works as,

> George Crable, "The Borough" (1810).
> Charles Kingsley, *Yeast* (1848); *Alton Locke* (1850).
> Elizabeth Gaskell, *Mary Barton, A Tale of Manchester Life* (1848).

Swift and Addison and Steele are closer to Smith in their positive view of the businessman. Heilbroner has pointed out that Smith did not foresee "the ugly factory system."[14] By describing the reactions of ordinary people to the Industrial Revolution, literature can fill in the gaps of much writing about economics.

# Footnotes

[1]Joseph Addison and Richard Steele, *Selections from the Tatler and the Spectator,* ed. Robert J. Allen (New York: Holt, Rinehart and Winston, 1957), pages 120, 121.

[2]*Ibid.,* p. 63.

[3]A scholar of my acquaintance has suggested seriously that the last two are now being done by American scientists.

[4]G. B. Harrison, ed., *Major British Writers,* Vol. I. (New York: Harcourt, Brace and Co., 1959), p. 641.

[5]*Ibid.,* p. 642.

[6]The poems relating to Wood's half-pence listed in Jonathan Swift, *Poetical Works,* ed. Herbert Davis (London: Oxford University Press, 1967), are,

> "A Serious Poem upon William Wood"
> "An Epigram on Wood's Brass-Money"
> "To his Grace the Arch-Bishop of Dublin"
> "An Excellent New Song Upon His Grace Our good Lord Archbishop of Dublin"
> "Prometheus"
> "Whitshed's Motto on his Coach"
> "Verses on the upright Judge"
> "Horace, Book I, Ode XIV, paraphrased and inscribed to Ireland"
> "Wood, an Insect"
> "On Wood the Iron-Monger"
> "A Simile on our Want of Silver"

[7]All quotations of the poem are from: Wylie Sypher, ed., *Enlightened England.* rev. ed. (New York: W. W. Norton and Co., Inc., 1962).

[8]The third entry in *The Oxford English Dictionary* for "wealth" cites this poem as an example of usage. It means, "Prosperity consisting in abundance of possessions; 'worldly goods', valuable possessions, esp. in great abundance; riches, affluence" (page 3718). An older meaning of *wealth,* now obsolete, is "2. Spiritual well-being." It appears, then, that Goldsmith is contrasting the older meaning to the newer meaning, showing the absence of spiritual values in the 'sons of wealth.'

[9]The word *luxury* had a stronger meaning than it has at present: "1. Lasciviousness, lust . . . Obsolete" *(O.E.D.,* p. 1683).

[10]Robert L. Heilbroner, *The Worldly Philosophers*. 4th ed. (New York: Simon and Schuster, 1972), p. 60.

[11]Adam Smith, *The Theory of Moral Sentiments*, Part I, section 1, Chapter 1, in: *Enlightened England*, p. 1219.

[12]Edmund Burke, *Reflections on the Revolution in France* in: *Enlightened England*, pages 1246-1247.

[13]Jonathan Swift, *Poetical Works*, "The Run upon the Bankers," lines 49-51, page 194. The other poem is "The Bank thrown down," page 221.

[14]Heilbroner, page 70.

Bartleby

# CHAPTER FIVE

### Herman Melville, "Bartleby the Scrivener:
### A Story of Wall Street"

This short story was first published anonymously in 1853 in *Putnam's Monthly Magazine*. The main character is Bartleby, a scrivener employed by a law firm on Wall Street. The narrator is Bartleby's employer. Other characters include Nippers and Turkey, two other scriveners, and Ginger-Nut, an office-boy. Although the story is set in a law office, it is reasonable to consider this a story with a business setting. The narrator describes himself as ". . . one of those unambitious lawyers who never address a jury . . . but, in the cool tranquillity of a snug retreat, do a snug business among rich men's bonds and mortgages, and title-deeds."[1]

Although the story has implications about the nature of evil and about God's will, business is a topic in itself, and a metaphor for farther-reaching human problems. The first footnote in the Norton Anthology edition reveals the editors' view of Melville's attitude toward business:

> Like Bartleby, [Melville] also distrusted the economic compulsions of society . . . . The other two scriveners, Turkey and Nippers, support the conventional system of the law and the profits, and their reward is

paid in neuroses, alcoholism, ulcers, and unacknowl-
edged envy of Bartleby's superiority.[2]

Bartleby is presumed superior because he rejects profits. It
should be pointed out, however, that Bartleby never makes his
motives clear. He never launches into a direct attack on the business community or the profit motive. Neither does Melville. Nor
is it clear that the narrator is an evil capitalist. Interpreters have
seen the narrator as a cruel, scheming individual, who is at least
partly responsible for Bartleby's withdrawal from the world, and
death. However, it seems to me that the narrative shows the
narrator to be a good-hearted man, who makes serious attempts
to understand and befriend Bartleby. Bartleby never reveals his
feelings to anyone, and is unreachable; in modern terminology,
Bartleby might be viewed as very neurotic or schizophrenic. The
narrative does not seem to me to be a white-wash either: it shows
the development of the narrator's feelings, and does not dwell on
a justification of his motives. It is important at the outset of this
chapter to place this story in perspective. Many readers make the
general assumptions found in the footnote quoted above. It is
certainly true that Bartleby is seen in contrast to the business
world. It is not clear, however, that all business is condemned,
and Bartleby heroized.

This chapter will concentrate on aspects of the story that
characterize business and businessmen. Recognizing that Melville is using Wall Street and business as a vehicle for a treatment
of more serious matters, I have isolated six negative qualities of
business developed in the story by Melville. First, Bartleby is
fired because of "necessities connected with my business,"[3] and
this after the narrator says Bartleby has "affected" him "in a
mental way."[4] Second, by analogy to Caius Marius, Bartleby has
been betrayed after commendable service. Third, Wall Street
hides misery, and is false in its appearance. Fourth, Wall Street is
cold and impersonal. Fifth, Wall Street confines, walls in, and
isolates. These characterizations about Wall Street can be assumed to apply to business in general. Sixth, there is a generally
monolithic and funereal atmosphere surrounding Bartleby.

Bartleby came in answer to an advertisement. With some
hindsight, the narrator describes Bartleby's first appearance at

his office: "I can see that figure now — pallidly neat, pitiably respectable, incurably forlorn!"[5] In his first days there, Bartleby proves to be a very good worker: "he seemed to gorge himself on my documents."[6] He is also described as working ". . . silently, palely, mechanically." On his third day, Bartleby is asked to verify the accuracy of his copy, and replies, "I would prefer not to." Several days later, Bartleby gives the same reply to a similar request. The narrator describes his reaction:

> With any other man I should have flown outright into a dreadful passion, scorned all further words, and thrust him ignominiously from my presence. But there was something about Bartleby that not only strangely dis-armed me, but, in a wonderful manner, touched and disconcerted me. I began to reason with him.[7]

There is here a consideration of Bartleby's feelings, absurd as his behavior appeared. Following this, the narrator asked the other employees what they thought of the incident, and all saw no justification for Bartleby's reaction. "But once more business hurried me. I determined again to postpone the consideration of this dilemma to my future leisure."[8]

The narrator continued to postpone a direct decision about Bartleby. The "evil impulse" once got the better of the narrator, and he lost his temper with Bartleby. "As days passed on, I became considerably reconciled to Bartleby. His steadiness, his freedom from all dissipation, his incessant industry (except when he chose to throw himself into a standing revery behind his screen), his great stillness, his unalterableness of demeanor under all circumstances, made him a valuable acquisition."[9] After con-sidering Bartleby a dilemma, the narrator became reconciled to Bartleby in light of his hard work. There is a strong implication here that the narrator has judged Bartleby on the basis of his value as an employee, rather than in a more general moral con-text.

After some time passes, Bartleby resolves to do no more copy-ing, but remains in the office. The narrator says he felt "sorry" for Bartleby.

> In plain fact, he had now become a millstone to me,
> not only useless as a necklace, but afflictive to bear
> .... At length, necessities connected with my busi-
> ness tyrannized over all other considerations. De-
> cently as I could, I told Bartleby that in six days' time
> he must unconditionally leave the office.[10]

It seems fair to say that the major reason Bartleby was fired was
that he ceased to be a valuable employee. The narrator expresses
his sorrow for Bartleby to create a favorable impression of himself. Like businessmen today, the narrator does not enjoy firing
someone. Here is the opening paragraph of a *Fortune* article on
firing:

> Next to getting the ax, there is no more dreaded expe-
> rience in the corporate world than wielding it. The
> overwhelming majority of businessmen, belying their
> public image as cold and ruthless, get sick to their
> stomachs at the thought of having to tell a subordinate
> and colleague — often a close friend — that he's
> through.[11]

The phrasing of the narrator's remarks appears defensive. He
never explains the "necessities." Considering that the narrator
regarded Bartleby as a dilemma, and that Bartleby "touched"
him, the narrator's decision to fire Bartleby is not placed in the
most favorable context. The reader's sympathies may lie with
Bartleby. In addition, there is a promise of personal interest that
remains unfulfilled. While Bartleby works hard, the dilemma is
postponed. When Bartleby ceases to work, necessities develop.
    The general impression created by the narrator is that he felt
guilty about Bartleby, and that in his narrative he has attempted
to explain his actions by reference to good intentions and to business necessities over which he has no control. Yet, after Bartleby
refuses to leave the office, the narrator offers him $20. The inade-
quacy of business reasons in firing Bartleby is made clear when
the narrator finds himself ". . . recalling the divine injunction: 'A
new commandment give I unto you, that ye love one another.'"[12]
It can be concluded, then, that Melville has placed Bartleby's

firing for business reasons in an unfavorable context. These business necessities mock deeper spiritual considerations.

The second negative characterization of business is that
Bartleby is unrewarded for and betrayed after his hard work and
loyal service. Finding Bartleby in the office on a Sunday morning,
the narrator thinks: "And here Bartleby makes his home; sole
spectator of a solitude which he has seen all populous — a sort of
innocent and transformed Marius brooding among the ruins of
Carthage!"[13] A footnote to the Norton Anthology edition describes Caius Marius as a ". . . plebian general and consul of
Rome, after notable victories in Africa, betrayed by patricians
and exiled, became a popular figure of nineteenth-century democratic literature and art." In a sense more general, the narrator
never faces the "dilemma" directly, and beneath his expressions
of sorrow for Bartleby is the conviction: "Rid myself of him, I
must; go, he shall."[14]

The third unfavorable characterization of business is that Wall
Street (and business in general) hides misery, and so, presents a
false image. The contrast of Bartleby's misery to the gala appearance of those at Trinity Church (next to Wall Street) on a Sunday
morning is a revelation to the narrator:

> The bond of a common humanity now drew me ir-
> resistably to gloom. A fraternal melancholy! For both I
> and Bartleby were sons of Adam. I remembered the
> bright silks and sparkling faces I had seen that day, in
> gold trim, swan-like sailing down the Mississippi of
> Broadway; and I contrasted them with the pallid
> copyist, and thought to myself, Ah, happiness courts
> the light, so we deem the world is gay; but misery
> hides aloof, so we deem that misery there is none.[15]

This thought follows the discovery that Bartleby lives in the office
at night. This is the first time Bartleby is seen outside his work
environment. The implication is that the business world requires
a false appearance, one which does not tolerate misery. In the
article by Herbert Meyer, referred to earlier, executives who
have been fired are advised to conform in their appearances, to

look young, and to present themselves as ". . . walking solutions to a company's problems."[16]

Although a positive appearance is advised by "de-hiring" firms, Melville sees this as falseness. The gaiety of the business world is false because it hides misery. In addition, the narrator's actions are in doubt. At one point, the narrator finds "content" by reading spiritual works about predestination.[17] Later, he tries to persuade Bartleby to accept another position because he is "Fearful, then, of being exposed in the papers."[18] Although the narrator's feelings are mixed, a desire to maintain an appropriate appearance is a motivating force.

A fourth consideration, similar to the third, is that Wall Street (and business in general) is cold and impersonal. Immediately before the analogy to Caius Marius (page 935), the narrator considers the contrast of the daily activity of Wall Street with the nightly and week-end emptiness of the place. He uses such words as "deserted," "emptiness," "sheer vacancy," and "forlorn." Wall Street is compared to the ruins of Carthage. Later, the narrator moves his offices in an attempt to rid himself of Bartleby. When the screen, the last piece of furniture, is removed, Bartleby is ". . . the motionless occupant of a naked room."[19]

The fifth negative characterization of business, related to the third and fourth, is that Wall Street (and business) confines, walls in, and isolates. While considering Bartleby's strange dissociation from others, the narrator is reminded of the murder of Samuel Adams by John C. Colt in 1842.

> Often it had occurred to me in my ponderings upon the subject that had that altercation taken place in the public street, or at a private residence, it would not have terminated as it did. It was the circumstance of being alone in a solitary office, up stairs, of a building entirely unhallowed by humanizing domestic associations — an uncarpeted office, doubtless, of a dusty, haggard sort of appearance — this it must have been which greatly helped to enhance the irritable desperation of the hapless Colt.[20]

There is a clear implication that business offices are devoid of warmth, and that they isolate the occupant. Later in the story, the narrator suggests that Bartleby work as a clerk in a drygoods store, and he replies, " 'There is too much confinement about that.' "[21] Early in the story, after Bartleby's second refusal to check his copy, the narrator comments, "Meanwhile Bartleby sat in his hermitage, oblivious to everything but his own peculiar business there."[22] Bartleby also made a habit of staring out the window in a "dead-wall revery."[23] Although Melville is concerned with Bartleby's unique and enigmatic predicament, there is a strong implication that Wall Street itself has fostered his isolation and confinement.

It is assumed by many recent writers about business that the impact of environment on the psychological condition of workers has been perceived only recently. To express this view, here is a quotation from the textbook used in a required M.B.A. course at New York University in the Fall of 1976:

> In recent years, there has been increasing recognition of the often "hidden," but significant, impacts that physical settings can have on organizational behavior.
>
> . . . physical settings may influence a variety of functions and may often be a necessary condition, even if an insufficient condition, for optimal work motivation and achievement.[24]

Melville's narrator was aware of such influences, and Melville apparently intended his readers to believe that such impacts were significant.

The sixth unfavorable characteristic of the business world is the generally monolithic and funereal atmosphere surrounding Bartleby. Bartleby's psychological problems may be said to encourage this view, but the business world itself shares some of the responsibility. The new occupant of the narrator's offices has Bartleby arrested when he refuses to leave. There is a grim, funereal sense to the arrest: ". . . the silent procession filed its way through all the noise, and heat, and joy of the roaring thoroughfares at noon."[25] Bartleby is sent to the Tombs, a Manhattan prison, which has since been closed. He faces the wall, and refuses food. The description of the prison yard resembles the negative implications of Wall Street:

The yard was entirely quiet. It was not accessible to the common prisoners. The surrounding walls, of amazing thickness, kept off all sounds behind them. The Egyptian character of the masonry weighed upon me with its gloom. But a soft imprisoned turf grew under foot. The heart of the eternal pyramids, it seemed, wherein, by some strange magic, through the clefts, grass-seed, dropped by birds, had sprung.[26]

This resembles the description of Wall Street on Sunday morning. It is followed by a reference to Bartleby as having worked in the Dead Letter Office in Washington: "Dead letters! does it not sound like dead men?"[27] These dead letters, the narrator says, contain ". . . pardon for those who died despairing; hope for those who died unhoping; good tidings for those who died stifled by unrelieved calamities." There is an implied similarity between the dead letters and Bartleby's work on Wall Street, and, beyond that, to Wall Street and business in general. In addition, the analogy of Egyptian architecture, which is nearly synonymous with silence and funerals, can be assumed to extend beyond the Tombs to Wall Street and to business in general.

Both the narrator and Bartleby are complex individuals. There is no simple cause and effect between business and the moral stances of either of the story's main characters. A final interpretation of Bartleby is very difficult. He might be seen as heroic, but he might also be seen as pathetic or as repulsive. The narrator describes the progress of his own feelings:

My first emotions had been those of pure melancholy and sincerest pity; but just in proportion as the forlornness of Bartleby grew and grew to my imagination, did that same melancholy merge into fear, that pity into repulsion.[28]

Nor is it clear that Melville expected a clear, single emotion about Bartleby to arise in the reader. The narrator explains that ". . . it was his soul that suffered, and his soul I could not reach."[29] Nor is a final interpretation of the narrator easy to form. He may be genuinely sympathetic, but he may also be defensive, and too vain to reach out to Bartleby.

Hence, an ultimate conclusion about Melville's characterization of business and businessmen is also difficult. The first argument, that business reasons occupy too large a place in the narrator's feelings, is a serious charge. This may explain the narrator's defensiveness and desire to avoid Bartleby. It is not clear that the narrator attempts to love his neighbor, even though he accepts the principle. However, it may be argued that this is true of all men, and did not arise in the narrator because he works on Wall Street. His last words are, "Ah, Bartleby! Ah, humanity!"

The negative implications about Wall Street, its falseness, its coldness, its isolation, and its similarity to the pyramids, may be seen as Melville's manner of creating an appropriate tone for the story. (Melville was born near Wall Street.) Furthermore, the narrator recognizes these negative characteristics. So, there is not an implication that businessmen cannot recognize the meaning of their experiences. At this point, it can be concluded that the view of the story expressed by the Norton Anthology editors (in their first footnote) that Bartleby is superior to Turkey and Nippers, and that he distrusts the economic compulsions of society is too strong. There is, however, criticism of those aspects of business — including its architecture — which encourage isolation, falseness, and an absence of Christian love.

## Footnotes

[1] Herman Melville, "Bartleby the Scrivener: A Story of Wall Street" in: *The American Tradition in Literature*, ed. Sculley Bradley, Richard Croom Beatty, and E. Hudson Long. Vol. I, 3rd ed. (New York: Grosset and Dunlap, Inc., 1967), p. 922.

[2] *Ibid.*, p. 921.

[3] *Ibid.*, p. 939.

[4] *Ibid.*, p. 938.

[5] *Ibid.*, p. 927.

[6] *Ibid.*

[7] *Ibid.*, p. 929.

[8] *Ibid.*, p. 930.

[9] *Ibid.*, p. 933.

[10]*Ibid.*, pages 939-40.

[11]Herbert E. Meyer, "The Fluorishing New Business of Recycling Executives," *Fortune*, XCV, No. 5 (May, 1977), p. 328.

[12]*Melville*, p. 943.

[13]*Ibid.*, p. 935.

A different view of Caius Marius from the one mentioned in the Norton Anthology footnote appears in *Helping the Troubled Employee* by Joseph F. Follmann, Jr. N.Y.: AMACOM, 1978: "In his later years, the Roman consul Caius Marius is described as being extraordinarily sick, subject to nocturnal frights and auditory hallucinations, and despondent" (p. 15).

[14]*Ibid.*, p. 945.

[15]*Ibid.*, p. 935.

[16]Meyer, p. 338.

[17]Melville, p. 944.

[18]*Ibid.*, p. 947.

[19]*Ibid.*, p. 946.

[20]*Ibid.*, p. 943.

[21]*Ibid.*, p. 948.

[22]*Ibid.*, p. 930.

[23]*Ibid.*, p. 944.

[24]Don Hellriegel and John W. Slocum, Jr., *Organizational Behavior Contingency Views* (St. Paul: West Publishing Co., 1976), pages 342-3.

[25]Melville, p. 949.

[26]*Ibid.*, p. 951.

[27]*Ibid.*, p. 952.

[28]*Ibid.*, p. 936.

[29]*Ibid.*

# CHAPTER SIX

## Conclusion

This book has investigated the works of fourteen writers from the thirteenth to the nineteenth century: Dante, Chaucer, Gower, Langland, Shakespeare, Marlowe, Milton, Goldsmith, Swift, Addison and Steele, Smith, Burke, and Melville. As noted in the introduction, this book is reasonably complete through the eighteenth century, focusing on English literature. Melville is the only American, and the only nineteenth century author included. The last two centuries have seen a great increase in works dealing with business and the businessman: Dickens, Dreiser, Fitzgerald, and Miller, are examples. An appendix lists English and American works dealing with business and businessmen from the beginning to the present. I would like to suggest that the major patterns delineated in this book can also be found in English and American literature of the last one hundred seventy-eight years.

The works studied here range from the view that businessmen are all bad to a mixed view — some businessmen are bad and some are good. Seven of the fourteen — Dante, Gower, Langland, Marlowe, Swift, Goldsmith, and Melville — are hard on businessmen. It is significant that the earliest and the latest writers take the same general view of business and businessmen. Three others — Chaucer, Shakespeare, and Swift — present a mixed view of businessmen; but each of the three expresses a negative view of businessmen. Chaucer's Merchant is an unhappy pilgrim, and there are innuendos that he is a usurer and cheater. The merchant in "The Shipman's Tale," and the Parson's remarks in his tale soften this view somewhat. Shakespeare's Shylock is, regardless of attempts to sentimentalize him, a thoroughly evil, merciless usurer. However, Bassanio and Antonio are good merchants. In *The Drapier's Letters,* Swift is hard on English monetary policy, but accomplishes his purpose in the guise of a businessman. Milton, Addison and Steele, Smith, and Burke have been studied through essays about business. Thus, an image of the businessman must be abstracted. Milton is favorable to free commerce, or trade not controlled by a king, but has strong moral reservations about businessmen. Addison and Steele admire the energy of Sir Andrew Freeport, a merchant, who is seen as a non-violent empire-builder: ". . . for true Power is to be got by Arts and Industry."[1] Even Burke and Smith are tentative about business and businessmen! Burke opposed the confiscation of property following the French revolution: "Few barbarous conquerors have ever made so terrible a revolution in property."[2] Yet, he was not in agreement with the moral positions of economic politicians: "Even commerce and trade and manufacture, the gods of our economical politicians, are themselves perhaps but creatures, are themselves but effects which, as first causes, we choose to worship."[3] Burke regarded the system of trade and manufacture in eighteenth century England as an outgrowth from "ancient manners," especially Christian virtues and learning. Smith also regarded his economic system as bounded by religious and moral principles. Hence, within a *laissez-faire* system of free trade individual participants would be ordered by their Christian consciences.[4]

The overall image of the businessman is negative. To some extent all of these writers, except Addison and Steele, express denunciation of businessmen and their motives. The charge of usury is made by Dante, Chaucer, Gower, Langland, Shakespeare, Marlowe, and by implication, Swift. In 1869 the Debtor's Act abolished imprisonment for debt in England. The power of creditors over debtors must have been used ruthlessly in many instances in preceding centuries.[5] With the rise of the merchants,

74

and later, Calvinism and the reaction against Calvinism, the specific charge of usury declined. Business was for a time regarded as an aid to the development of the middle class. However, the assumption was that businessmen were morally good, and would not abuse free trade. Goldsmith is the only author included here who presents a humanistic reaction against the cruelty of the Industrial Revolution. Numerous later writers followed Goldsmith in reacting against this movement. Sinclair's *The Jungle,* Norris's *The Octopus,* and Dickens' *Hard Times* are notable examples. Both usury and the evils of the Industrial Revolution are similar in the charges made against businessmen. In *The Jungle,* Jurgis, the excessively hard worker, is described as the sort of man the bosses complain they do not find enough of. In *Hard Times,* Coketown is devoid of human emotion, and reveals only what is "severely workful." "Bartleby the Scrivener" also depicts the business world as devoid of human kindness, and as a destroyer of the human spirit. In *Hard Times,* Bounderby, a businessman, and Gradgrind, a teacher, are close friends, and both are described as "devoid of sentiment." (Two of Gradgrind's sons are named Adam Smith and Malthus.) Is Bounderby a better man than Shylock or than one of Dante's usurers? It seems fair to conclude that there is a tradition within which the businessman is seen as exerting cruel power over others, either by usury, or through the factory system of the Industrial Revolution.

A second major theme discovered in these works is the businessman as *pavenu.* Chaucer and Goldsmith are good examples. In more recent literature, Bounderby in *Hard Times,* Silas Lapham in *The Rise of Silas Lapham,* and Babbitt in *Babbitt* are excellent examples of this. The narrator of "Bartleby the Scrivener" may fit into this category. Although I do not see him as an evil figure, it is true that he loves wealth, yet has difficulty with generosity; and he is a successful lawyer, but finds justice perplexing in the case of Bartleby. This charge against businessmen derives in part from their status as a rising class. Bounderby is consistently contrasted to Mrs. Sparsit's good breeding. She mentions her familiarity with the opera at an early age. He replies, "E-gad, ma'am, so was I — with the wrong side of it. A hard bed the pavement of its arcade used to make, I assure you."[6] The other part of this charge derives from the view that businessmen have an insatiable desire for wealth, at the expense of wisdom. Chaucer's Franklin, Goldsmith's "sons of wealth," and Melville's narrator reveal this. Another example is Henry Worthington Cowperwood in Dreiser's *The Financier,* who was careful of what he said and whom he talked to because he "wanted to get ahead socially and financially." Babbitt's "god was Modern Appliances." *Goodbye, Columbus* by Philip Roth indicates that this theme has not disappeared.

A third major charge, and the most serious of all, is that business and businessmen are devoid of Christian virtue. Only Addison and Steele, and Smith do not exhibit this view, because, I think, they stress an optimistic view of human desires. Shylock is devoid of mercy; Langland's merchants do not pay attention in church;[7] Goldsmith's businessmen destroy established virtues; Milton's traders may value luxury. In "Bartleby the Scrivener," Melville considers free will and fate in the character of Bartleby and in his relationship with the narrator, and the description of Wall Street makes it cold and deathlike — devoid of Christian love. T. S. Eliot's description of London in "The Burial of the Dead" in "The Waste Land" is similar in tone. Death of the soul and commerce as a basis for war are implied.

> Unreal city,
> Under the brown fog of a winter dawn,
> A crowd flowed over London Bridge, so many,
> I had not thought death had undone so many.
> Sighs, short and infrequent, were exhaled,
> And each man fixed his eyes before his feet.
> Flowed up the hill and down King William Street,
> To where Saint Mary Woolnoth kept the hours
> With a dead sound on the final stroke of nine.
> There I saw one I knew, and stopped him, crying:
>     "Stetson!
> "You were with me in the ships at Mylae!
> "That corpse you planted last year in your garden,
> "Has it begun to sprout? Will it bloom this year?
> "Or has the sudden frost disturbed its bed?
> "Oh keep the Dog far hence, that's friend to men,

"Or with his nails he'll dig it up again!
"You! hypocrite lecteur! — mon semblable —
   mon frère!"
   (Lines 60-76)

Elizabeth Drew's notes suggest that Stetson is "probably a symbol for the average businessman." Professor Leonard Albert of Hunter College interprets Stetson to mean 'let the sun stand;' Stetson has buried a corpse, a grotesque perversion of fertility. Professor Albert also interprets the reference to Saint Mary Woolnoth to mean that man is kept in time and not released to eternity.[9] Eliot's statement that the passage is influenced by *Inferno* III, 55-57, and IV, 25-27, in which Dante and Virgil shun the spiritually empty, lends credence to Professor Albert's interpretation. In lines 74 and 75, Dog seems to be God backwards (used also by George Barker), and the nails suggest Christ on the Cross. In tone this passage resembles Langland and Gower, and was influenced by the *Inferno*.

What of the positive aspects of the businessman in literature? Addison and Steele saw him as a gatherer of national wealth and power. Milton believed that God favored free commonwealths and free trade over kingdoms. Swift moved the Irish to political opposition to the English through the guise of a drapier. Smith and Burke defended the gathering of wealth and property as a basic right of English-speaking people, and explained and defended free enterprise and industrialization.

In concluding, I wish to raise two further questions: exactly why have writers been hard on business and businessmen and what will the future hold for businessmen in literature? In answering the first question, it is fair to say that literature fills in the gaps of economic history as that is usually practiced. In *The Worldly Philosophers* Heilbroner does not discuss "The Deserted Village," and presents a rather superficial view of *The Theory of Moral Sentiments*. In *Money* Galbraith does not refer to *The Drapier's Letters* or to Wood's half pence. Literature tells us how the human heart regarded great economic movements, a service no businessman should do without. I still have not said *why* businessmen are portrayed as evil in many literary works. The medieval view of usury is a good example. The standard view is

77

that the Church, which one professor I had said "dominated the world in the Middle Ages," said no and that made usury wrong. Let me present an analogy. *The Wall Street Journal,* Jan. 16, 1979 reported that the government in Afghanistan banned "usurious moneylending . . . but lenders won't lend at reasonable rates." The issue does not relate to charging interest per se, but to the oppression of other people through unreasonable interest rates. In chapter two it was shown that complaints about usury softened from Dante to Chaucer, but all writers studied complained about the thraldom that these lender-borrower relationships could bring. Nothing has changed in this regard since the thirteenth century. Anyone who destroys virtue or crushes his fellow man in business is evil. We still have people who do this; those who do it with excessive interest rates are called loansharks or Shylocks.

Similarly, wealth itself is not evil, it is the love of worldly things above the love of one's fellow man that is evil. Too often, Adam Smith is regarded as an advocate of *laissez-faire* and some of the less humanistic consequences of it. In fact, Smith believed that the business world and the impulse for profit would be tempered by the businessman's sympathy for his fellow man. Smith was somewhat optimistic, but it is at least essential that the modern businessman understand that Smith did not encourage wealth for its own sake or an unscrupulous profit motive. Only by a Christian regard for others could the profit motive be a good thing. It is because of the all too frequent absence of this moral tempering of the profit motive that businessmen have received harsh treatment in literature.

We may expect the same human concerns to appear in future literature about businessmen. Some writers will become obsessed with wealth itself or usury, but those who know humanity best will not hesitate to vilify anyone who makes another person his thral through money.

I hope the literary student has gained a fuller appreciation of the richness and importance of the businessman in literature, and that the businessman has gained a fuller understanding of the place of business in this society and of his own place in the business community.

# Footnotes

[1] Joseph Addison and Richard Steele, *Selections from the Tatler and the Spectator*, ed. Robert J. Allen (New York: Holt, Rinehart & Winston, 1965), p. 63.

[2] Edmund Burke, *Reflections on the Revolution in France* (New York: Doubleday and Co., Inc., 1961), p. 129.

[3] Edmund Burke, *Reflections on the Revolution in France* in: *Enlightened England*, ed. Wylie Sypher. rev. ed. (New York: W. W. Norton & Co., Inc., 1962), p. 1246.

[4] Burke refers to the "natural effect" of the violence in France as intended "to shock the *moral sentiments* of all virtuous and sober minds" [italics mine], Burke, *op. cit.*, p. 137.
Addison and Steele, e.g., Steele's *The Conscious Lovers*, and Goldsmith also emphasize the importance of moral sentiments.

[5] William Lewis, historian for the U.S. Army Southern Command, headquartered in the Panama Canal Zone, informed me in 1970 that the Carcel Modello in Panama City is largely a debtor's prison. This suggests that the power of creditors over debtors remains strong outside the English-speaking countries.

[6] Charles Dickens, *Hard Times* (New York: Bantam Books, 1964), p. 67.

[7] This theme appears in I, i of "The Merchant of Venice."
> Salarino: . . . Should I go to Church
> And see the holy edifice of stone,
> And not bethink me straight of dangerous rocks,
> Which touching but my gentle vessel's side,
> Would scatter all her spices on the stream,
> Enrobe the roaring waters with my silks,
> And, in a word, but even now worth this,
> And now worth nothing?
> (Lines 29-36).

[8] T. S. Eliot, "The Waste Land," ed. Elizabeth Drew in: *Major British Writers*, ed. G. B. Harrison. Vol. II (New York: Harcourt, Brace & World, Inc., 1959), p. 832.

[9] Professor Leonard Albert, lectures in "Contemporary Literature," Hunter College, 1966.

[10] Although not chosen for close analysis in this book because the main character is not a businessman, *Robinson Crusoe*, according to Ian Watt in *The Rise of the Novel* (Berkeley: University of California Press, 1957), "give[s] narrative expression to the ideological counterpart of the Division of Labour, the Dignity of Labour" (p. 73).

# APPENDIX

## WORKS CONCERNING
## THE BUSINESSMAN
## IN LITERATURE

This appendix lists all literary works known to me in which the businessman appears prominently, and appropriate secondary sources. Most of these works have been referred to in this book.

Addison, Joseph and Richard Steele. *Selections from the Tatler and the Spectator*. Ed. Robert J. Allen. New York: Holt, Rinehart and Winston, 1957.

Addison, Joseph and Richard Steele. *The Tatler and the Spectator*. (1709–1712).

*American Public Addresses 1740–1952*. Ed. A. Craig Baird. New York: McGraw Hill, 1956.

*The American Tradition in Literature*. Eds. Sculley Bradley, Croom Beatty, and E. Hudson Long. 3rd ed. Vol. I. New York: Grosset and Dunlap, Inc., 1967.

Auchincloss, Louis. *The Embezzler*. (1966).

St. Augustine, *De Civitate Dei*. (426).

Baumback, Clifford M., Kenneth Lawyer, and Pearce C. Kelley. *How to Organize and Operate a Small Business*. 5th ed. Englewood Cliffs: Prentice Hall, Inc., 1973.

Bellamy, Edward. *Looking Backward*. (1888).

Bellow, Saul. *Henderson the Rain King*. (1959).

Black, Henry Campbell. *Black's Law Dictionary*. 4th ed. St. Paul: West Publishing Co., 1951.

Bloomfield, Morton. *The Seven Deadly Sins*. Michigan: University of Michigan Press, 1952.

Boethius, *De Consolatione Philosophiae*. (c. 524).

Burgum, Edwin Berry. "Theodore Dreiser and the Ethics of American Life." in: *The Novel and the World's Dilemma*. New York: Oxford University Press, 1947.

Burke, Edmund. *Reflections on the Revolution in France*. (1790).

Carlyle, Thomas. *Sartor Resartus*. (1833-34).

Chaucer, Geoffrey. *The Canterbury Tales*. (1387-1400).

*Chaucer: Modern Essays in Criticism*. Ed. Edward Wagenknecht. New York: Oxford University Press, 1959.

Chaucer, Geoffrey. *The Works of Geoffrey Chaucer*. Ed. F. N. Robinson. 2nd ed. Boston: Houghton Mifflin Company, 1961.

*The Compact Edition of the Oxford English Dictionary*. Eds. C. T. Onions, et. al. Oxford: Oxford University Press, 1971.

Crabbe, George. "The Village." (1783): "The Borough." (1810).

*Cursor Mundi*. (c. 1300).

Dante. *La Divina Commedia*. (c. 1307-1321).

Dante. *The Portable Dante*. Ed. Paolo Milano. New York: The Viking Press, 1947.

Dante. *Dante Alighieri: Tutte Le Opere*. Ed. Fredi Chiappelli. Milano: U. Mursia & Co., 1965.

Dante. *The Divine Comedy of Dante Alighieri: Inferno*. Ed. John D. Sinclair. New York: Oxford University Press, 1939.

Dante. *The Divine Comedy of Dante Alighieri: Il Purgatorio*. Ed. John D. Sinclair. New York: Oxford University Press, 1939.

Defoe, Daniel. *Robinson Crusoe*. (1719).

de Perrault, Guillaume. *Summa de Vitiis; Summa de Virtutibus*. (before 1261).

Dickens, Charles. *Hard Times*. (1854); *Domby and Son*. (1847-48).

Dreiser, Theodore. *The Financier*. (1912); *The Titan* (1914); *The Stoic* (1947).

Drucker, Peter F. *The Effective Executive*. New York: Harper and Row, Publishers, 1967.

*Enlightened England: An Anthology of English Literature from Dryden to Blake*. Ed. Wylie Sypher. Rev. Ed. New York: W. W. Norton and Co., Inc., 1962.

Ewing, David W. *Freedom Inside the Organization*. New York: E. P. Dutton, 1977.

Ewing, David W. *The Managerial Mind*. New York: The Free Press, 1964.

Fitzgerald, F. Scott. *The Last Tycoon*. (1940).

Forbes, Allyn B. "The Literary Quest for Utopia, 1880-1900." *Social*

*Forces,* IV (Dec. 1927), 179–189. (General information on "utopian" fiction, including such works as Charles Sheldon's *In His Steps.*)

Franklin, Benjamin. *The Autobiography.* (1771, 1784).

Galbraith, John Kenneth. *Money.* New York: Bantam Books, 1975.

Galsworthy, John. *The Forsyte Saga.* (1922).

Gardner, Ralph D. *Horatio Alger, or The American Hero Era.* Mendota, Ill.: Wayside Press, 1964.

Garland, Hamlin. *A Son of the Middle Border.* (1914).

Gaskell, Elizabeth. *Mary Barton, a Tale of Manchester Life.* (1848).

Gingrich, Arnold. *Business and the Arts: An Answer to Tomorrow.* New York: Paul S. Ericksson, Inc. 1969.

Goldsmith, Oliver. "The Deserted Village." (1770); *The Vicar of Wakefield.* (1766).

Gower, John. *Confessio Amantis.* (1390–92).

Gower, John. *The English Works of John Gower.* Ed. G. C. Macaulay. London: Oxford University Press, 1969 rpt.

Haskins, Charles Homer. *The Renaissance of the Twelfth Century.* Cambridge: Harvard University Press, 1953.

Heer, Friedrich. *The Medieval World.* Trans. Janet Sondheimer. New York: The New American Library, 1961.

Heilbroner, Robert L. *The Worldly Philosophers.* 4th ed. New York: Simon and Schuster, 1972.

Heller, Joseph. *Catch-22.* (1955). Ch. 29 on bureaucracy.

Hellriegel, Don and John W. Slocum, Jr. *Organizational Behavior Contingency Views.* St. Paul: West Publishing Co., 1976.

Holman, C. Hugh. *Goldentree Bibliographies: The American Novel Through Henry James.* New York: Appleton-Century-Crofts, 1966. (Excellent bibliography on major and minor novelists.)

Hopkins, Gerard Manly. "God's Grandeur." (c. 1880).

Howells, William Dean. *The Rise of Silas Lapham.* (1885).

Hyman, Stanley Edgar. "Melville the Scrivener." *NMO,* XXIII (1953), 381–415.

Pope Innocent III. *De Miseria Humanae Conditionis.* (c. 1216). Translated in Bernard Murchland.

Kavesh, Robert A. *Businessmen in Fiction: The Capitalist and Executive in American Novels.* Hanover, New Hampshire: The Amos Tuck School, Dartmouth College, 1955.

Kingsley, Charles. *Yeast.* (1848); *Alton Locke* (1850).

Kittredge, George Lyman. *Chaucer and His Poetry.* Cambridge: Harvard University Press, 1915.

Klingerman, Charles. "The Psychology of Herman Melville." *Psychoanalytic Review,* XL (1953), 125–143.

Langland, William. *Piers Plowman.* (c. 1362 ff.).

Langland, William. *The Vision of William Concerning Piers the Plowman In Three Parallel Texts*. Ed. Walter W. Skeat. London: Oxford University Press, 1969 rpt.

Lawrence, D. H. *Women in Love*. (1921). Ch. 17 "The Industrial Magnate."

Lewis, Charlton T. and Charles Short. *A Latin Dictionary Founded on Andrews' Edition of Freund's Latin Dictionary*. Oxford: The Clarendon Press, 1879.

Lewis, C. S. *The Discarded Image*. Cambridge: Cambridge University Press, 1964.

Lewis, Sinclair. *Babbitt*. (1922).

*A Literary History of England*. Ed. A. C. Baugh. New York: Appleton-Century-Crofts, 1967.

Lorens, Frere. *Somme de Vices et Vertus*. (1279). Add also Richard Brunne. *Handlying Synne*. (1303).

Lynn, Kenneth S. *The Dream of Success: A Study of the Modern American Imagination*. Boston: Little, Brown, 1955. (Deals with Dreiser, Norris, Alger, and others.)

*Major British Poets*. Ed. Oscar Williams. New York: The New American Library, 1963.

*Major British Writers*. Gen. Ed. G. B. Harrison. II Vols. New York: Harcourt, Brace and Co., 1959.

Marlowe, Christopher. *Five Plays*. Ed. Havelock Ellis. New York: Hill and Wang, 1956.

Marlowe, Christopher. "The Jew of Malta." (1633).

McGalliard, John C. "Characterization in Chaucer's *Shipman's Tale*." *Philological Quarterly*, LIV, No. 1 (Winter, 1975), 1–18.

Melville, Herman. "Bartleby the Scrivener: A Story of Wall Street." (1853).

Meyer, George Wilbur. "A New Interpretation of *The Octopus*," *CE*, IV (1943), 351–359.

Meyer, Herbert E. "The Flourishing New Business of Recycling Executives." *Fortune*, XCV, No. 5 (May, 1977), 328–338.

Meyers, A. R. *England in the Late Middle Ages (1307–1536)*. Middlesex, England: Penguin Books Ltd., 1952.

Miller, Arthur. "All My Sons." (1947); "The Death of a Salesman." (1949).

Millgate, Michael. "Theodore Dreiser and the American Financier." *SA*, VII (1961), 133–145.

Milton, John. "The Ready and Easy Way to Establish a Free Commonwealth." (1660).

Milton, John. *Complete Poems and Major Prose.* Ed. Merritt Y. Hughes. New York: The Odyssey Press, 1957.

Moliere. "The Miser." (1668).

Morgan, H. Wayne. "William Dean Howells: The Realist as Reformer." in: *American Writers in Rebellion from Twain to Dreiser.* New York: Hill and Wang, 1965. (Good also on Frank Norris, Theodore Dreiser, Hamlin Garland, and Mark Twain.)

Murchland, Bernard, trans. *Two Views of Man.* New York, 1966.

Noble, David W. "Dreiser and Veblen and the Literature of Cultural Change." in: *Studies in American Culture: Dominant Ideas and Images.* Ed. Joseph J. Kwiat and Mary C. Turple. Minneapolis: University of Minnesota Press, 1960.

Oates, J. C. "Melville and the Manichean Illusion," *TSLL,* IV (1962), 117–129.

Odets, Clifford. "Waiting for Lefty." (1935); "Awake and Sing." (1935).

Ovid. *Metamorphoses.* (c. 8 A.D.).

Pennafort, Raymond of. *Summa Casuum Poenitentiae.* (c. 1235).

Pirenne, H. *Medieval Cities.* Princeton: Princeton University Press, 1925.

Pizer, Donald. "Synthetic Criticism and Frank Norris; or, Mr. Marx, Mr. Taylor, and *The Octopus,*" *AL,* XXXIV (1963), 532–541.

*The Pricke of Conscience.* (c. 1340).

Roth, Philip. *Goodbye, Columbus.* (1959).

Shakespeare, William. "Pericles." (1608); "The Merchant of Venice." (1597).

Shakespeare, William. *Complete Works.* Ed. Hardin Craig. Chicago: Scott, Foresman and Co., 1961.

Shaw, George Bernard. "Man and Superman." (1903).

Sidney, Sir Philip. "The Defense of Poesy." (1595).

Sinclair, Upton. *The Jungle.* (1906); *King Coal.* (1917); *Oil!* (1927).

Smith, Adam. *Theory of Moral Sentiments.* (1759); *The Wealth of Nations.* (1776).

Smith, Adam. *The Wealth of Nations.* In *Enlightened England: An Anthology of English Literature from Dryden to Blake.* Ed. Wylie Sypher. Rev. Ed. New York: W. W. Norton and Co., Inc., 1962.

Smith, Adam. *Theory of Moral Sentiments* (1759). London: A. M. Kelley, 1967.

*Sources and Analogues of Chaucer's Canterbury Tales.* Eds. W. F. Bryan and Germaine Dempster. Chicago: University of Chicago Press, 1941.

Spenser, Edmund. *The Faerie Queene.* (I–III 1590; IV–VI 1596).

Steinbeck, John. *The Grapes of Wrath.* (1939).

Swift, Jonathan. *The Drapier's Letters.* (1724).

Swift, Jonathan. *Poetical Works.* Ed. Herbert Davis. London: Oxford University Press, 1967.

Taylor, Walter F. *The Economic Novel in America.* Chapel Hill: University of North Carolina Press, 1942. Reviewed by Lyon N. Richardson in: *American Literature.* XIV, 440–443. (Taylor concentrates on Twain, Garland, Bellamy, Howells, and Norris, but does not mention Melville.)

Taylor, Walter F. "On the Origin of Howells' Interest in Economic Reform." *AL*, II (1930), 3–14. (Same author who wrote *The Economic Novel in America.*)

Taylor, Walter F. "William Dean Howells and the Economic Novel." *AL*, IV (1932), 103–113.

Tebbel, John. *From Rags to Riches: Horatio Alger, Jr., and the American Dream.* New York: Macmillan, 1963.

Thoreau, Henry David. *Walden.* (1854).

Thrall, William Flint and Addison Hibbard. *A Handbook to Literature.* Rev. C. Hugh Holman. New York: The Odyssey Press, 1960.

Tillyard, E. M. W. *The Elizabethan World Picture.* New York: Vintage Books, no date.

Toynbee, Arnold J. *A Study of History.* An abridgement of Volumes I to VI by D. C. Somervell. New York: Oxford University Press, 1947.

*Tudor Poetry and Prose.* Eds. J. William Hebel, et. al. New York: Appleton-Century-Crofts, Inc., 1953.

Vergil. *Aeneid.* Ed. Charles Knapp. Chicago: Scott, Foresman and Company, 1923.

Virgil. *Aeneid.* (29–19 B.C.).

Waller, Leslie. *The Banker.* (1965).

Watt, Ian. *The Rise of the Novel.* Berkeley: University of California Press, 1957.

Wilson, Sloan. *The Man in the Gray Flannel Suit.* (1955).

Witte, Karl. *Essays on Dante.* Trans. C. Mabel Lawrence and Philip H. Wicksteed. London, 1898.

Wordsworth, William. "The Old Cumberland Beggar." (1800).